# Using an ISA Mobile App for Professional Development

Graham Passmore • Julie Prescott

# Using an ISA Mobile App for Professional Development

palgrave
macmillan

Graham Passmore
Lakehead University
Thunder Bay, ON, Canada

Julie Prescott
Department of Psychology
University of Law
Manchester, UK

Dr. Prescott would like to thank the 'University of Bolton Jenkinson Fund' for monies that were used to generate the mobile App that is introduced in this book.

ISBN 978-3-030-99070-1     ISBN 978-3-030-99071-8  (eBook)
https://doi.org/10.1007/978-3-030-99071-8

© The Author(s), under exclusive licence to Springer Nature Switzerland AG 2022
This work is subject to copyright. All rights are solely and exclusively licensed by the Publisher, whether the whole or part of the material is concerned, specifically the rights of translation, reprinting, reuse of illustrations, recitation, broadcasting, reproduction on microfilms or in any other physical way, and transmission or information storage and retrieval, electronic adaptation, computer software, or by similar or dissimilar methodology now known or hereafter developed.
The use of general descriptive names, registered names, trademarks, service marks, etc. in this publication does not imply, even in the absence of a specific statement, that such names are exempt from the relevant protective laws and regulations and therefore free for general use.
The publisher, the authors and the editors are safe to assume that the advice and information in this book are believed to be true and accurate at the date of publication. Neither the publisher nor the authors or the editors give a warranty, expressed or implied, with respect to the material contained herein or for any errors or omissions that may have been made. The publisher remains neutral with regard to jurisdictional claims in published maps and institutional affiliations.

Cover illustration: Pattern © Melisa Hasan

This Palgrave Macmillan imprint is published by the registered company Springer Nature Switzerland AG.
The registered company address is: Gewerbestrasse 11, 6330 Cham, Switzerland

*To Phoebe and Jacob, love Mummy*

## Contents

1  A Review of the ISA Method — 1

2  The Indeterminate Identity Variant — 31

3  The Defensive High Self Regard Identity Variant — 55

4  The Diffuse High Self-Regard Identity Variant — 77

5  The Crisis Variant — 93

6  The Defensive Negative Variant — 107

# LIST OF FIGURES

| | | |
|---|---|---|
| Fig. 1.1 | App Splash page | 10 |
| Fig. 1.2 | Hit the + sign to create a new instrument | 11 |
| Fig. 1.3 | The instrument creation interface | 12 |
| Fig. 1.4 | An empty construct text box | 13 |
| Fig. 1.5 | The completed instrument interface | 14 |
| Fig. 1.6 | Login page | 15 |
| Fig. 1.7 | Accessing the instrument for data entry | 16 |
| Fig. 1.8 | Demographic data entry | 17 |
| Fig. 1.9 | Instrument completion | 18 |
| Fig. 1.10 | The saved instrument | 19 |
| Fig. 1.11 | Opening Ipseus interface | 24 |
| Fig. 1.12 | The entity pane | 24 |
| Fig. 1.13 | The construct pane | 25 |
| Fig. 1.14 | The display pane | 25 |
| Fig. 1.15 | The participant pane | 26 |
| Fig. 1.16 | The analysis pane | 26 |
| Fig. 2.1 | Representation of the ISA identity variants of the identity of Chap. 2 | 34 |
| Fig. 2.2 | Demarcation of identity variants | 35 |
| Fig. 2.3 | ISA parameter ranges for the identity of Chap. 2 | 36 |
| Fig. 2.4 | Constructs of low and high SP | 38 |
| Fig. 2.5 | Constuct detail | 38 |
| Fig. 2.6 | Raw scores | 44 |
| Fig. 2.7 | Empathetic identification pattern | 45 |
| Fig. 2.8 | Conflicted identification pattern | 47 |
| Fig. 3.1 | Demarcation of identity variants | 58 |

| | | |
|---|---|---|
| Fig. 3.2 | Raw ratings | 59 |
| Fig. 3.3 | Raw scores | 60 |
| Fig. 3.4 | Representation of the ISA identity variants of the identity of Chap. 3 | 70 |
| Fig. 4.1 | Representation of the ISA identity variants of the identity of Chap. 4 | 86 |
| Fig. 5.1 | Representation of the ISA identity variants of the identity of Chap. 5 | 101 |
| Fig. 6.1 | Representation of the ISA identity variants of the identity of Chap. 6 | 116 |

# List of Tables

| | | |
|---|---|---|
| Table 2.1 | Core and conflicted values and beliefs | 39 |
| Table 2.2 | Idealistic and contra identifications | 43 |
| Table 3.1 | Core and conflicted values and beliefs | 61 |
| Table 3.2 | Idealistic and contra-identifications | 63 |
| Table 3.3 | Raw scores: idealistic identification | 64 |
| Table 3.4 | Raw scores: contra-identification | 65 |
| Table 3.5 | Raw scores: conflicted identification | 68 |
| Table 4.1 | Core and conflicted values and beliefs | 79 |
| Table 4.3 | Raw scores: idealistic identification | 81 |
| Table 4.2 | Idealistic and contra-identifications | 81 |
| Table 4.4 | Raw scores: contra-identification | 82 |
| Table 4.5 | Raw scores: conflicted identification | 84 |
| Table 5.1 | Core and conflicted values and beliefs | 95 |
| Table 5.3 | Raw scores: idealistic identification | 96 |
| Table 5.2 | Idealistic and contra-identifications | 96 |
| Table 5.4 | Raw scores: contra-identification | 97 |
| Table 5.5 | Raw scores: conflicted identification | 100 |
| Table 6.1 | Core and conflicted values and beliefs | 109 |
| Table 6.2 | Idealistic and contra-identifications | 110 |
| Table 6.3 | Raw scores: idealistic identification | 111 |
| Table 6.4 | Raw scores: contra-identification | 112 |
| Table 6.5 | Raw scores: conflicted identification | 114 |

# CHAPTER 1

# A Review of the ISA Method

**Abstract** The aims of this book are to provide the reader with an understanding of Identity Structure Analysis (ISA); how to use the new ISA App, as well as how to interpret and make use of the report generated by the Ipseus software for the purposes of counselling and professional development. This chapter introduces ISA and the Weinreich template that was developed to guide analysis. This chapter also introduces counselling supervision and a nascent counselling supervision instrument that researchers wishing to investigate ISA and counselling supervision might develop further. Through the introduction of this new counselling supervision instrument, we hope the chapter will provide readers with a useful starting point for the development of their own ISA instrument(s). The Appendix to this chapter reviews the Ipseus software and introduces a mobile app. Ipseus was developed for ISA data collection and IS report creation using a PC. The mobile app was designed and developed by the authors to enable ISA data collection using tablets and mobile phones (ISA report creation is not possible using the app). Later chapters of the book use the Weinreich template to build on our prior work (Passmore, Turner, & Prescott, Identity structure analysis and teacher mentorship: Across the context of schools and the individual. Palgrave, 2019) by providing tables taken from Ipseus reports. The goal in providing such tables is to further the reader's understanding of our approach to analytic interpretation.

© The Author(s), under exclusive license to Springer Nature Switzerland AG 2022
G. Passmore, J. Prescott, *Using an ISA Mobile App for Professional Development*, https://doi.org/10.1007/978-3-030-99071-8_1

**Keywords** Identity structure analysis • Weinreich template • Counselling • Supervision • Counseling supervision instrument • Mentoring • Ipseus • Mobile App • ISA instrument • Bipolar constructs • Entities

## Introduction

As a starting point, this chapter will give a brief background to ISA and its goals. This brief discussion sets the scene for the presentation of an illustrative description of the process we undertook to develop the counselling supervision instrument that we created in order to develop and test the ISA mobile app. Description of the process of developing the counseling supervision instrument ought to serve as a starting point for the reader who wishes to develop a(n) instrument(s) of their own. In our earlier work (Passmore et al., 2019), we considered the use of ISA for teacher mentorship and considered how ISA can help guide the mentoring process. Throughout this earlier work, we argued how the detail ISA can reveal might support the mentoring process by providing the mentor with insights the mentee may not have considered. We also argued that this insight may provide the mentor with information about concerns the mentee already has such that mentorship might lead to resolution. Finally, we noted that it might be the case that ISA provides insight that the mentee refutes in mentorship sessions. Regardless of the status that the insights hold for the mentee, we argued that they can become a starting and focal point for mentee sessions. When looking at trainee teachers, we focussed on mentoring; in later chapters of this work, we will consider using insights derived from ISA report analysis for the purposes of counselling supervision. That is, Chaps. 2, 3, 4, 5 and 6 will focus on how ISA can support the professional development of an individual through counselling supervision.

With the nature of ISA, and instrument creation presented, this chapter terminates with a tutorial that covers use of Ipseus, an extant software dedicated to ISA data collection and report creation. Ipseus was designed for use on a PC or laptop. The chapter also provides a tutorial for a new mobile app and links to download it. The app was developed by the authors for ISA data collection with small-screen technologies. It encourages the use of smaller instruments than has typically been the case for ISA studies. Relative to large instrument completion on a PC with Ipseus, the app aims to make ISA data collection more engaging, more accessible, and less time consuming. We have piloted the app and feedback suggests it achieves these initial aims. We hope the app, which is free to download and use from Googleplay and the App store, will be utilised by researchers interested in using ISA.

## Goals of ISA

In Weinreich (2003), identity is defined as 'the structural representation of the individual's existential experience, in which the relationships between self and other agents are organized in relatively stable structures over time, but which become elaborated and changed on account of new experiences' (p. 1). In Passmore et al. (2019), we provided a description of Weinreich's ISA method. Our goal in taking a descriptive approach was to better convey the nature of the ISA method and its associated approach to data analysis. In this book, we stick with the descriptive tack as we still feel that it is useful for guiding academics toward familiarity with the ISA method (a major goal of this work).

In addition to a description of the ISA method, this chapter provides a description of a template that Weinreich developed to standardise and expedite the analysis of ISA reports. The template considers the nature of the most used and salient ISA parameters and provides pointers for the application of these parameters in the analytic process. In Passmore et al. (2019), we built on the template by including a consideration of raw scores that are used by the Ipseus software to calculate idealistic, contra and conflicted identification parameters of identity (among other parameters). In Chap. 2, we re-describe our approach to ISA analysis using a set of theoretical data that largely conforms to the desired indeterminate ISA identity variant. In Chap. 2 also, images are taken from the ISA report that Ipseus generated for the hypothetical indeterminate identity. The images illustrate how raw data and subsequently calculated parameter values appear in an Ipseus report. Description of the process of interpreting raw data and parameter values as provided in the images is used to enhance (relative to the understanding that is made available in Passmore et al., 2019) reader comprehension. In later chapters, hypothetical raw scores for other identity variants are similarly placed in tables to further meet our goal of improving reader comprehension of our approach to ISA report and data analysis.

The raw data of Chap. 2 and later chapters was collected with the mobile app. Introducing the app is another goal of this chapter (and of the book). A tutorial that describes entering an instrument (and subsequent data collection) into the mobile app is provided in the Appendix to this chapter as is a tutorial that considers the use of Ipseus. The instrument that is entered into the app in the tutorial is described in the body of this chapter as a nascent ISA counselling supervision instrument. Chapters 2, 3, 4, 5 and 6 describe the use of the instrument and the app to meet the goal of (a process that continues in the remaining chapters of the book) describing how they might be applied in Professional Development (PD). That is, the app and the instrument are used to move us toward the realisation of another goal of the book, which is to consider the application of ISA for counselling supervision for the purposes of professional development. We first described this goal in the closing chapter of Passmore et al. (2019).

## ISA AND COUNSELLING SUPERVISION

As mentioned, in our previous work (Passmore et al., 2019), we discuss the value of using ISA as a mentoring tool with a focus on trainee teachers. In the concluding chapter of this previous publication, we considered the future of ISA for mentoring and professional development with a focus on how ISA could be beneficial for counselling supervision. There are many definitions of supervision dependent on the profession and country. A frequently quoted definition of supervision by Bernard and Goodyear (2004) states; *'supervision is an intervention provided by a more senior member of a profession to a more junior member of that same profession. This relationship is evaluated, extends over time and has the simultaneous purposes of enhancing the professional functioning of the more junior person, monitoring the quality of professional services offered to the clients seen and serving as a gatekeeper for those who are to enter the particular profession (2004, p. 8)*. Supervision has been defined by the British Psychological Society (BPS) Division of Counselling Psychology as *'designed to offer multi-level support in an atmosphere of integrity and openness for the purpose of enhancing reflective skills, maximising the effectiveness of therapeutic interventions, informing ethical decisions and facilitating an understanding of the use of self'* (2005, p. 5). Within the counselling profession, supervision forms a number of functions, aside from professional development. Supervision can be an avenue to monitor ethical or behavioural concerns (Bernard & Goodyear, 2014; Paige & Wosket, 2015). as well as allow time and a place for the discussion of any emotional support needs (De Stefano et al., 2007). Supervision is viewed by the British Association for Counselling and Psychotherapy (BACP) as a crucial aspect underpinning professional practice, vital in supporting practioners in adhering to the ethical framework in the UK (BACP, 2002). The BACP requires all accredited counsellors to have supervision whereas in the USA, supervision is only conducted with trainee therapists (Wheeler, 2003). Supervisors tend to hold a number of roles, including that of mentor and teacher (Morgan & Sprenkle, 2007), with one important aim of supervision with trainee counsellors particularly being to help in their identity development (Watkins, 2017). According to Watkins (2017), there are two preeminent supervision principles. These two principles are

1. Create a forever enabling and empowering space that galvanises supervisee learning and
2. Tailor supervision to match supervisee developmental learning needs (p. 146).

We believe that ISA could help both of these principles on a continuing basis and allow for a deeper knowledge of pressing factors to address issues the supervisee may be unaware need addressing within themselves (Passmore et al., 2019).

Watkins and colleagues (Watkins Jr. et al., 2015; Watkins Jr. & Scaturo, 2013) put forward that supervision should be a place/setting that allows both education and healing for the supervisees (See Watkins, 2017). Watkins (2017) identified '*50 (non-exhaustive) commonalities shared by any and all supervision perspectives that cut across 9 practice impacting areas*' (p. 140). The impacting areas being supervisee characteristics, supervisor qualities, supervisee change processes, supervision structures, supervision relationship elements, supervision common principles, supervisor tasks, supervisor common roles, and supervisor common practices (p. 140). It is proposed that some of these 50 commonalities could potentially be used to help researchers design and develop the ISA components that may need addressing. Indeed, in designing the counselling supervision instrument used in this book to showcase the mobile app, we considered these 9 practice areas which informed the interview schedule (more on this shortly).

In addition, Watkins (2017) argues that the counselling profession could advance the practice of supervision by attending to its essential instructional and learning processes. Utilising ISA within supervision could allow supervisors to apply a structured framework to the supervision and allow supervisors and supervisees to explore issues that arise (Passmore et al., 2019). Watkins (2017) identifies the supervisee change process as having the following common factors: opportunity for catharsis/sharing, anxiety, distress and tension reduction, activation of self-observation, self-reflection and insight development, exposure and confrontation of learning problems, acquisition and practice of new learning, success and mastery of new knowledge and skills (p. 144). As we did in the previous work (Passmore et al., 2019), we would like to suggest that including ISA within supervision could be useful in helping both parties identify areas where change may need to occur. The ISA process could be beneficial for supervisees as it may highlight a concern the supervisee had but found difficult to articulate to a supervisor for whatever reason. This would give space for the issue to be raised and to be addressed. Also, the ISA process could help a supervisor direct their supervision sessions based on the needs and concerns of the supervisee. It is evident that supervision plays an important role in the development of counselling practitioners with benefits including identity development, reduction in role conflict and role ambiguity (Inman et al., 2014), enhanced self-awareness, treatment knowledge, skills acquisition and utilisation, as well as self-efficacy (Hill & Knox, 2013; Wheeler & Richards, 2007; Wilson et al., 2016). However, the supervision relationship is viewed as important, with research considering what factors contribute to a successful supervision relationship (Watkins, 2017).

In the concluding chapter of Passmore et al. (2019), we suggested that ISA could provide supervisors and supervisees with a structured framework to the supervision process, in a similar vein to how we posit that ISA can provide the trainee teacher with a structured mentoring process. We designed the counselling supervision instrument outlined in this chapter (and as used throughout this publication) to also help illustrate the mobile app, based on this idea.

## The Development of a New ISA Instrument

As part of this book, we would like to encourage researchers interested in using ISA and the mobile app to gain an initial understanding of how to develop an ISA instrument to meet their needs. ISA instruments generally consist of an equal (or roughly equal) number of entities and bipolar constructs. Bipolar constructs represent components of the various themes (principal constructs that constitute an issue) that make up an ISA instrument. Entities are the people and institutions that influence a particular issue. ISA dictates that a number of required entities be present in an instrument and it allows for the inclusion of additional entities to accommodate comprehensive consideration of the issue in question. Both entities and bipolar constructs are selected for inclusion in the instrument in response to: the researcher's understanding of the topic of interest, a search of the literature and interviews involving persons of pertinence to the investigation that is to be conducted.

It is the case that the bipolar constructs align to themes that comprise the topic of interest. The counselling supervision instrument was developed with the three themes of normative function, formative function, and restorative function to supervision in mind (APA, 2014). The normative function focuses on the more managerial aspect of supervision which would include ethical and quality issues. A supervisor would help a supervisee monitor their own standards and spot any ethical considerations. The formative function focuses on a more educational and learning aspect of supervision. This educational function would be concerned with developing the supervisee in terms of knowledge, skills, attitudes and abilities. The third and final function is the restorative function, which would be concerned with the professional environment created by the supervisor that allows concerns and issues to be openly expressed and discussed in an environment that feels safe and respectful. Within this function, the supervisor would focus on the holistic wellbeing of the supervisee.

Based on these three functions to supervision, we then interviewed 3 trainee counsellors and 3 recently qualified counsellors to gain an insight into what they felt was important from the supervision process, the qualities they felt were important in a supervisor, and what they felt if anything was missing from their supervision. The interviews asked the following seven questions to help provide some insight and allowed us to then develop the instrument.

What approach does your supervisor take?
What are its strengths and weaknesses from your point of view?
Is there anything hard to talk about in supervision?
Does your supervisor help you stay within professional guidelines, and if so, how? If not, why do you think that is?
Does your supervisor help you to work through how you feel? If so, how, and if not, why do you think that is?
Does your supervisor help your professional development and in what ways?
What personal qualities make an effective/less effective supervisor?

It is important to note that this instrument, like the data we report on in this book, is hypothetical (in this case in the sense that the instrument has not been tested in the field). We offer the instrument as a starting point for researchers interested in applying their ISA to counselling supervision. Such researchers might wish to adapt and develop the instrument further for the purposes of their research.

ISA instruments consist of equal or roughly equal numbers of bipolar constructs and entities. The themes of the counselling supervision instrument are: normative, formative and restorative.

## The Counselling Supervision Instrument

### *Constructs*

*Formative Theme*

1. willing to learn ... closed to learning
2. is well-informed ... is poorly informed
3. shares knowledge ... doesn't share knowledge

*Normative Theme*

4. challenges ... never challenges
5. instructs ... encourages reflection
6. has strong boundaries ... struggles to keep boundaries
7. is creative ... sticks to the tried and tested
8. can be trusted ... cannot be trusted
9. always does it right ... makes mistakes

*Restorative Theme*

10. accepts ... judges
11. facilitates processing emotions ... leads to hiding emotions
12. adapts to my needs ... is quite rigid in approach
13. problem solves ... worries or avoids

### *Entities*

ISA seeks to reveal, in regard to the bipolar constructs of the instrument, the values and beliefs of entities of self and the perceived values and beliefs of non-self entities. Weinreich's template works to present these values and beliefs in a cohesive manner.

ISA instruments must include a number of required entities for example, Ideal Self, Contra-Ideal Self, Admired Person, and Disliked Person. These entities are considered to be universally evaluated in a positive (an ideal self and a person I admire) or negative (a disliked person and a contra-ideal self-entity) way. Additional required entities include entities of self that transcend biographic time (a past self, a present self and a future self). The latter entities and the remaining entities of the instrument are evaluated in ways that involve some combination of positive and negative ratings. The entities of our nascent instrument are presented below.

1. Me as I would like to be
2. Me as I would least like to be
3. Me as a trainee
4. Me as a professional
5. Me outside of work
6. Professional I admire
7. Professional I don't admire
8. Public figure I admire
9. Public figure I don't admire
10. Key adult female in my life (mother/female)
11. Key adult male in my life (father/male)
12. A good friend
13. A person I no longer like

The images below provide a brief illustration of the process of instrument creation in the mobile app. For a complete review of the process of entering an instrument into the app, please access the link to the tutorial that is provided in the Appendix to this chapter.

On opening the app, the first task is to identify oneself as a researcher or user (study participant). If one is logging in for the first time using the app, an account has to be created. Account creation is very simple and involves the same steps as most all apps (Fig. 1.1).

In Fig. 1.2 you can see that the Supervisor instrument in the app interface, indicating that it was the last instrument to be created in the app. The process of creating a new instrument is made possible by hitting the + sign that is presented at bottom left of the screen of Fig. 1.2.

Figure 1.3 illustrates the simple interface that the app makes available to the researcher for instrument creation. Begin by entering a title for the new instrument in the top text box. 'Supervision' has been entered in this

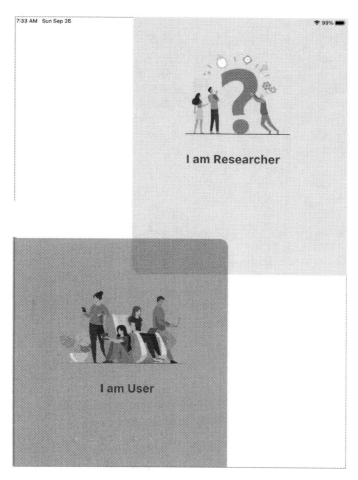

**Fig. 1.1** App Splash page

case. The next 2 text boxes call, in turn, for the researcher to enter a short description for the instrument and any instructions that need to be sent to study participants. When an instrument has been created, it is ready to be shared. At this point the app sends an invitation to study participants to complete the instrument. The email contains general instructions for instrument completion and links to download the app. The instruction in Fig. 1.3 to 'Please complete by Friday' is sent along with the above information. It represents an opportunity for the researcher to direct study

1 A REVIEW OF THE ISA METHOD   11

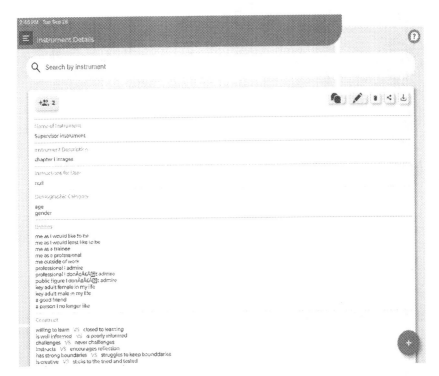

**Fig. 1.2** Hit the + sign to create a new instrument

participants in a manner that pertains to the instrument currently under consideration. The next 2 text boxes 'Age' and 'Gender' represent demographic category information that the researcher considers necessary for the study in question. Additional demographic categories are generated easily by the + sign that appears to the right of 'Age' in Fig. 1.3. Note that the − sign can be used to remove a demographic category. Entities and Constructs are entered into the instrument and removed in the exact same manner as demographic categories. Figure 1.4 illustrates how an empty construct text box is presented to the researcher after the + sign has been clicked.

The researcher continues adding entities and constructs until all of the components of the instrument have been entered into the app. The interface of Fig. 1.5 is presented to the researcher when the instrument is complete and the 'Save' button has been clicked.

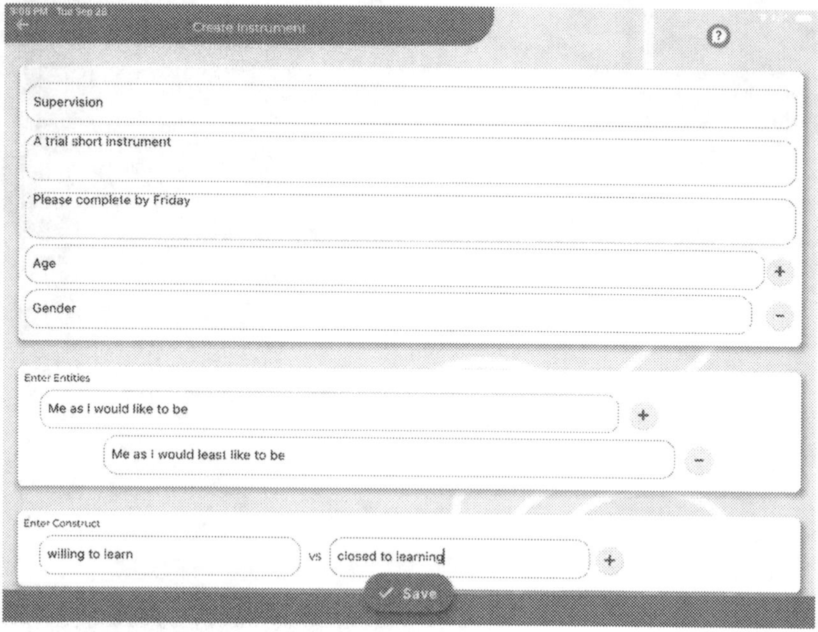

**Fig. 1.3** The instrument creation interface

Sharing the instrument with study participants begins with the researcher selecting the app 'share' icon at top right of the instrument, as seen in Fig. 1.5. Please note that the app tutorial goes over the processes of creating and sharing an instrument with study participants in greater detail.

Once an instrument has been shared, data entry (instrument completion) on the part of study participants can begin. In this and the following paragraph, we present our rationale for the creation of a mobile app to supplement data entry with Ipseus. Ipseus is a software that was created to accommodate ISA instrument creation, ISA data collection and, uniquely, ISA data analysis (screencap images and a link to a movie tutorial for Ipseus are provided in the Appendix of this chapter). When a study participant begins the completion of an instrument in Ipseus, the software creates a matrix of the bipolar constructs and entities of the instrument that is under consideration. Typical ISA instruments consist of 20 entities and 20 bipolar constructs. At the start of instrument completion, Ipseus generates a matrix of entities and bipolar constructs, it then presents each

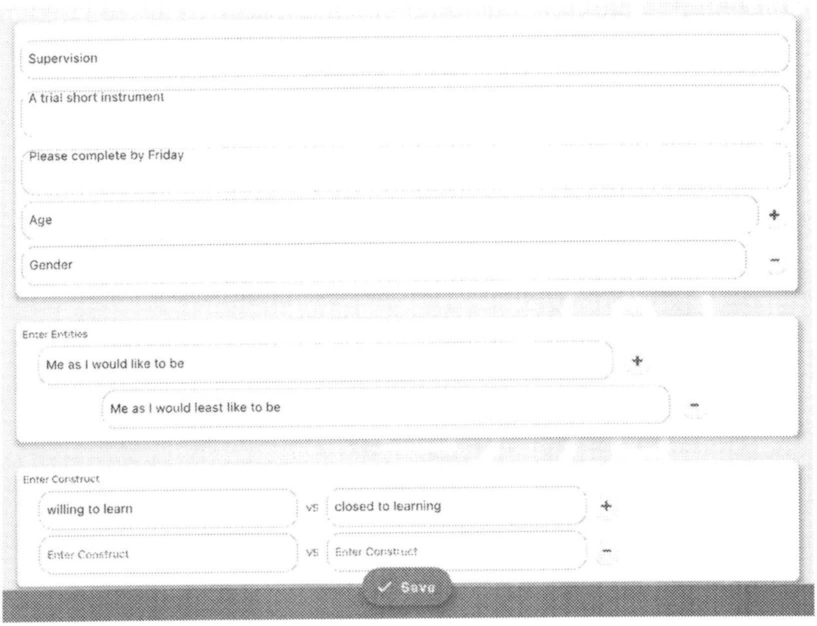

**Fig. 1.4** An empty construct text box

combination of entity and bipolar construct at random and in turn. On facing each combination of entity and construct, the participant ranks the entity along a 9-point (-4 to +4) scale according to their perception of that entity's stance toward the construct under consideration. This approach provides ISA with access to the participant's values and beliefs in an oblique manner. This indirect approach to the capture of values and beliefs is a cornerstone of the ISA method.

Once a study participant completes the matrix of entities and constructs, Ipseus converts the ratings into a set of raw scores. Ipseus then generates a set of quantitative values for the parameters of the ISA method. To do this, Ipseus inputs the raw scores into a series of formulae, each of which mathematically aligns to a description of an ISA parameter. The values are made available to the researcher as the 20-page Ipseus report. Ipseus can, at the researcher's discretion, generate reports for individuals (ideographic reports) or it can develop reports for groups of individuals within a study's population or indeed for the population of a study (nomothetic reports).

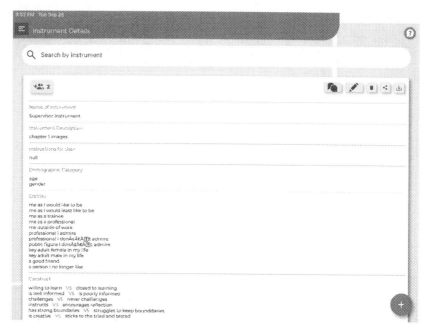

Fig. 1.5 The completed instrument interface

A considerable problem with data collection for 20 × 20 instruments is that entering 400 data points is both time consuming and mentally taxing (each data point is entered in the exact same way). Whereas Ipseus is designed for instrument creation and data entry using a PC, the app caters to the smaller screens of mobile phones and tablets; it also caters to smaller instruments. Our opinion is that catering to the popularity of smaller screens, by accommodating smaller instruments, by adding graphics and by adding sounds we might reduce the extent to which ISA data collection impinges on a study participant's time and mental stamina. The images below provide brief illustration of the process of data collection with the app. For full illustration of the processes of data collection with the app, please refer to the tutorial provided in the Appendix to this chapter.

The login page for study participants is essentially the same as the login page for researchers (Fig. 1.6). On entering standard information (for mobile apps), login is quickly enabled for the study participant at which point a page (Fig. 1.7) that provides access to the instrument is made available.

1  A REVIEW OF THE ISA METHOD    15

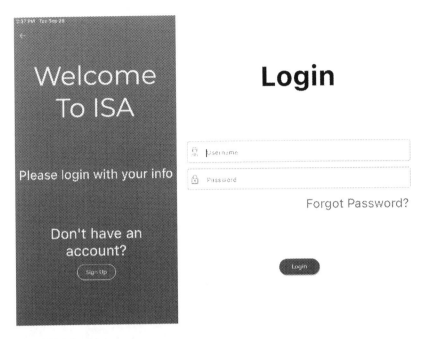

**Fig. 1.6** Login page

Figure 1.7 is of a screencapture image that was taken from a phone that gives access to more instruments than the average study participant will encounter. The check mark to the right of the clickable icon at the right of the screen indicates which instruments have been completed. The instrument that the study participant needs to access for the purposes of this text is the Supervisor instrument at the bottom of the screen. The study participant will know which instrument to complete as it is identified in the email that the researcher sends out on sharing the instrument.

On opening the Supervisor instrument, Fig. 1.8 indicates that the study participant's first task is to enter demographic information as requested by the researcher.

Figure 1.9 illustrates the screen that the study participant encounters on gaining access to the instrument. Figure 1.9 is rotated 90 degrees relative to Figs. 1.6 and 1.7 to illustrate that the screen can, and should be rotated, to best fit the instrument on the screen. On gaining access to a screen akin to Fig. 1.9, the study participant clicks on the first entity and makes a rating for the construct to hand (willing to learn Vs closed to

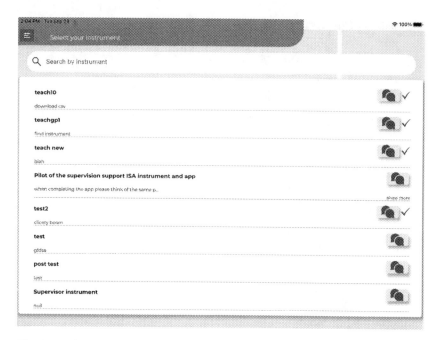

Fig. 1.7 Accessing the instrument for data entry

learning in this case). With the data so entered, the Next button at bottom right of the screen is clicked and the next bipolar construct is presented for rating purposes. Data is entered for all 13 constructs of the instrument in this manner, at which point the study participant selects the next entity of the instrument. 13 data points are entered again as before. The process continues until all 169 data points of the 13 × 13 matrix of entities and bipolar constructs have been entered into the app. At this stage, the study participant clicks the Save button, which sends the data onto the Researcher (Fig. 1.10).

Please note that the app prohibits moving onto the next entity of an instrument until all 13 data points have been entered. This facility assures that all of the data points of the instrument have been entered into the instrument before it can be saved.

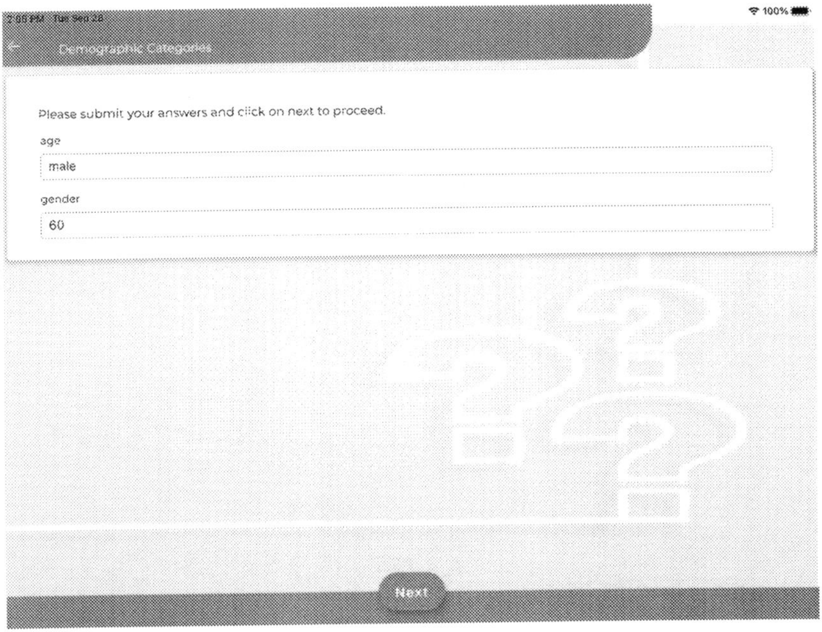

**Fig. 1.8** Demographic data entry

## The ISA Template

The information in a 20-page Ipseus report is extensive. Weinreich noticed that researchers struggled to focus on the most valuable information on offer. To offset this difficulty, he worked to develop a template that would expedite Ipseus report interpretation. In the text below, we describe the original template. In addition, we present Weinreich's description of the parameters that are most often used in ISA studies. We also present his consideration of how the parameters are to be interpreted and used in analytical reports (we edited his work at times to improve clarity). The template provides for step-wise consideration of the ISA parameters that are used most often in research studies (the most salient parameters). These parameters are described below in the order Weinreich recommended they be reported.

Fig. 1.9 Instrument completion

## The ISA Parameters of Concern

- Core and conflicted dimensions of identity.
- Idealistic and contra-identifications with influential others.
- Empathetic identifications for 2 current entities of self and one past entity of self.
- Identity conflicts for 2 current entities of self and one past entity of self.
- Evaluations of and ego-involvement with influential others.
- Evaluations of entities of self and identity diffusion.

### Parameter Descriptions and Tips for Use in an Analysis

Weinreich went beyond simply listing what he thought were the more salient parameters of the ISA method. He also provided a brief description

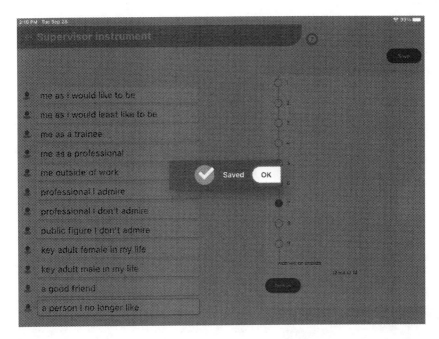

**Fig. 1.10** The saved instrument

of them along with tips for using them to generate standardised analyses of identities. Again, we have added to Weinreich's descriptions in the text below and edited his original text where we felt that doing so would improve clarity for the reader.

*Dimensions of Identity (the Person's Values and Beliefs)*
P13 of the Ipseus report contains a Construct Tabulation in which Structural Pressure is reported

1. **Core dimensions of identity**—Core dimensions of identity are those bipolar constructs with *high* (stabilising) magnitudes of Structural Pressure (SP). These are the dimensions that a person (or persons) use(d) to evaluate the merits of their social world (as outlined by the nature of the constructs of the identity instrument).

    N.B. The poles of the bipolar constructs represented in red represent the values, beliefs, characteristics and attributes that were endorsed as being positively aspirational. Being aspirational, they represent expected behaviours. It should be noted, however, that acting in full accordance with the noted values, beliefs and any concomitant behaviours will not necessarily be the case.

2. **Conflicted dimensions of identity**—Conflicted dimensions of identity are those bipolar constructs with *low* or *negative* magnitudes of SP. They are associated with contradictory appraisal of self and the social world such that a person's (or persons') actions may vacillate toward one pole or the other so that the likelihood for engaging in poor decision making is increased.

N.B. The black texts of bipolar constructs indicate the values, beliefs, characteristics and attributes that were endorsed as being negatively aspirational (though being non-aspirational, acting in full accordance with them will not necessarily be the case; they may not always be eschewed).

*Identifications with Other Agents, Groups and Societal Agencies*

Page 14 of the Ipseus report contains a Tabulation where the identification of role models is presented.

## *Aspirational Identification*

1. **Positive aspirational identification with others (idealistic-identification)**
Positive role models are identified on page 14 of the Ipseus report as the entities that are associated with significant idealistic identification. These entities are akin to the positive role models that the person (or persons) under consideration would wish to emulate.

2. **Negative aspirational identification with others (contra-identification)**
These are negative role models from which a person (or persons) would wish to dissociate.

## Empathetic Identification

Page 15 of the Ipseus report presents tabulation to indicate empathetic identification.

1. **Current empathetic identification based in 'Me, when I ... ... '** (referenced as CS1)
   With whom is empathetic identification close (high magnitudes)—in reporting note magnitudes with respect to 'entities of salient interest to the investigation'.
2. **Current empathetic identification based in 'Me, when I ... ...' (CS2)**
   Here again, note the entities of interest. Compare with the assessment above. Is there much in the way of modulation between these two states/contexts of identity? What does the evidence suggest about a person (or persons) when states/contexts change?
   N.B.: We have restricted our use of ISA to the above, but it would be possible to proceed with further CSs.
3. **Past (reconstructed) empathetic identification based in 'Me, ... ...'** i.e., *sometime in the past*
   Once again, report the entities of interest. Compare with the above assessments: Is there evidence of developmental/biographical change from *sometime in the past* to current or adult years? Consider the ways in which the modulation (changes in the entities with whom empathetic identification is prevalent) of empathetic identification from CS1 and CS2 and PS1 holds interpretive suggestions about the development of a person's (or persons) identity processes?

## Conflicts in Identification

P16 of the Ipseus report presents tabulation to indicate conflicted identification.

1. **Current identification conflict based in CS1**
   Note with whom identification conflict is the greatest and most problematic?
2. **Current identification conflict based in CS2**
   With whom is identification conflict the greatest and most problematic? What does the evidence suggest about differences between the two current states?

N.B.: Here again, we have restricted our use of ISA to the above CSs, but it would be possible to continue with any additional entities of current self.

3. **Past (reconstructed) identification-conflict based in PS1**
Compare with the above assessments: Is there evidence of developmental/biographical change from earlier to current or adult years. That is, has there been partial resolution of identification conflict or increasing identification conflict across the entities of the identification conflict pattern? Consider your thoughts regarding conflicted identification in relation to your interpretation of the patterns of empathetic identifications.

*Evaluation of, and Ego-Involvement with, Others (Individuals, Agencies, Groups, Etc.)*
P9 of the Ipseus report presents Entity Tabulation.

1. **Evaluation of, and ego-involvement with, entities of primary investigative interest**
Are these entities evaluated similarly or differently, and to what extent are they evaluated?

2. **Evaluation of, and ego-involvement with, other salient entities**
What is the ranking from the most favoured to the least favoured? Does ego involvement differ noticeably between them?

3. **Evaluation of, and ego-involvement with, societal institutions**
What are the perceived standings of these institutions (favoured or disfavoured)? Is ego involvement with them of minor/major extent.
    This evaluation and the remaining evaluations are not part of the counselling instrument.

4. **Evaluation of, and ego involvement with, representative entities of special interest**
How are these prototypical entities evaluated, and how intense is involvement with each?

5. **Evaluation of, and ego involvement with, parents**
For good or ill, parents (my mother, my father, or responsible agents) provide the all-pervading context for developmental and biographical experiences. How do they feature in respect of identity processes at the time of assessment?

## EVALUATION OF SELF AND EXTENT OF IDENTITY DIFFUSION

P6 of the Ipseus report presents Self Tabulation.

1. **PS1** *sometime in the past*
   Self-evaluation:
   Identity diffusion:
   Identity variant:
2. **CS1**
   Self-evaluation:
   Identity diffusion:
   Identity variant:
3. **CS2**
   Self-evaluation:
   Identity diffusion:
   Identity variant:

### *And Likewise for Other CSs*

Has self-evaluation increased from past to current self? When is self-evaluation most favourable and least favourable? Is identity diffusion relatively high, or low? Identity diffusion that is high indicates a tendency towards problematic issues in relation to identification conflicts (diffused identity variants). Identity diffusion that is low may denote defensive propensities (defensive identity variants).

### SUMMARY

Weinreich suggested concluding a template analysis with the provision of a holistic interpretation. He called for the interpretation to bear in mind all of the above findings. What is the overall assessment of current identity processes? What does this suggest about the societal realities in the current socio-historical context with which the identity under review relates, and the manner of agency in negotiating the complexities of these social realities? Do the findings indicate any obstacles to contributing to a fair democratic civil society; what might these be? Are there indications about procedures directed to identity processes that would mitigate against these resistances? In the chapters that follow we terminate template analyses with a holistic interpretation but prefer to reference it as a summary of the ISA report.

## Appendix

### *Ipseus Tutorial*

The first interface that the user encounters on opening the Ipseus software is provided below in Fig. 1.11.

Note how in the left-hand pane of the window, Ipseus invites you to enter a name for the instrument and also that it invites you to add the names of the instrument's author(s). Enter this information to start the instrument creation process. In the right-hand pane, the functions of interest are the entity and construct options. They enable the entry of the components of an ISA instrument into Ipseus. Figures 1.12 and 1.13

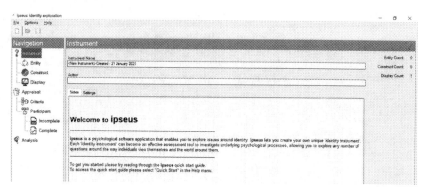

**Fig. 1.11** Opening Ipseus interface

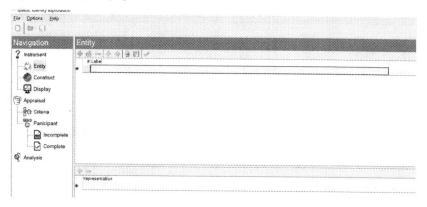

**Fig. 1.12** The entity pane

1 A REVIEW OF THE ISA METHOD    25

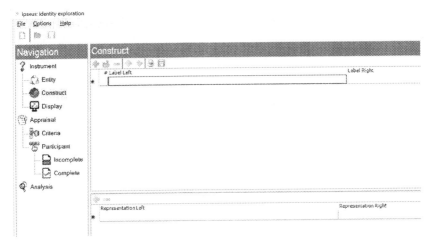

**Fig. 1.13** The construct pane

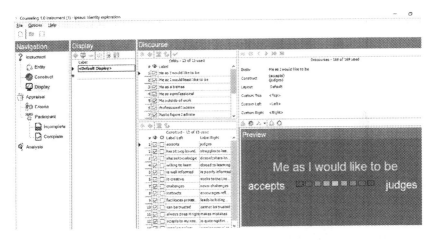

**Fig. 1.14** The display pane

portray the right-hand panes that these functions make available. Also of interest in this tutorial are the right-hand panes made available by the Display (Fig. 1.14), Participant (Fig. 1.15) and Analysis (Fig. 1.16) functions that can be seen in the left-hand pane of Fig. 1.11. Figures 1.12 and 1.13 portray the Ipseus interface before an instrument has been created. Figures 1.14, 1.15 and 1.16 portray the interface once an instrument has

26   G. PASSMORE AND J. PRESCOTT

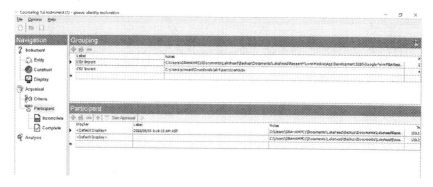

**Fig. 1.15** The participant pane

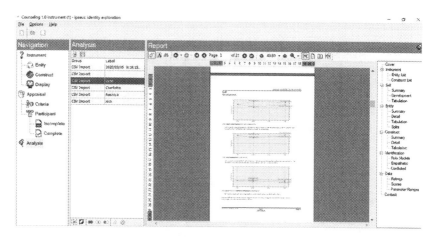

**Fig. 1.16** The analysis pane

been created. The link to the movie component of this tutorial indicates clearly and in depth how a user is to go about:

- creating and importing an instrument made in Ipseus;
- importing data collected with Ipseus and with the mobile App;
- the steps required to complete data analysis and generate an Ipseus report.

Link to the Ipseus movie tutorial

## App Tutorial

The mobile app was designed and developed by the authors to facilitate data collection from mobile phones and tablets. Part of the impetus for the design and creation of the app was to augment ISA's arsenal of data collection options; the Ipseus software, and a software called Participate (Participate, like the mobile app, serves as means for data collection only while Ipseus can be used for data collection and for data analysis). The mobile app adds to the data collection options for ISA in that Ipseus and Participate are laptop/PC based. The app further adds to the ISA data collection options in that the small screen size of mobile phones encourages the use of small ISA instruments. Typically, ISA instruments consist of 20 entities and 20 bipolar constructs. Completing a 20 × 20 instrument requires that a study participant make a point-selection on the screen 400 times. Each selection step (a tapping motion) is physically identical and requires a considerable measure of mental focus. Maintaining the mental concentration for the 40–45 minutes that 20 × 20 instrument completion requires is taxing and, we suggest, potentially off-putting. The use of smaller instruments may off-set much of the difficulty around maintaining mental focus by reducing the time for instrument completion. We additionally designed the app to facilitate rapid data entry (relative to Ipseus and Participate) by permitting data entry for all entities of an instrument against each bipolar construct in turn. This reduces the need to shift focus after making each data selection point in Ipseus and Participate where entity and construct combinations are presented to the participant at random until all 400 (20 × 20) data points have been entered. A goal of this work is to investigate the capacity that smaller instruments hold for elucidating aspects of an identity.

In closing, we will note the remaining stimuli for creating the mobile app. First, we wanted to offer a more engaging means for ISA data collection, and second, we wanted to provide for, and investigate the potential of ISA using short instruments. Typically, ISA instruments comprise a 20 × 20 matrix of entities and constructs. Entering 400 data points into Ipseus or Participate is a time-consuming and highly iterative process. We felt that an app, if suitably designed, could not only make the process of data entry more engaging, it might also make for better data as the engaged study participant is likely to be more focused. Further, while the app can accommodate an instrument of any size, we wanted to reduce the duration for which a participant has to concentrate on data entry. The new counselling instrument is abbreviated to a 13 × 13 matrix. Using a shortened ISA instrument allows investigation into a secondary goal of this work, which is to consider the capacity that short ISA instruments hold for detailed, and valuable, identity analyses.

Link to the App movie tutorial

## References

American Psychological Association. (2014). *Guidelines and Principles for Accreditation of Programs in Professional Psychology: Quick Reference Guide to Internship Programs*.

BACP. (2002). *Ethical framework for good practice in counselling and psychotherapy*. BACP.

Bernard, J. M., & Goodyear, R. K. (2004). *Fundamentals of clinical supervision*. Pearson.

Bernard, J. M., & Goodyear, R. K. (2014). *Fundamentals of clinical supervision* (5th ed.). Merrill.

British Psychological Society. (2005). *Division of counselling psychology: Professional practice guidelines*. British Psychological Society.

De Stefano, J., D'Iuso, N., Blake, E., Fitzpatrick, M., Drapeau, M., & Chamodraka, M. (2007). Trainees' experiences of impasses in counselling and the impact of group supervision on their resolution: A pilot study. *Counselling and Psychotherapy Research, 7*(1), 42–47. https://doi.org/10.1080/14733140601140378

Hill, C. E., & Knox, S. (2013). Training and supervision in psychotherapy. In M. J. Lambert (Ed.), *Bergin and Garfield's handbook of psychotherapy and behaviour change* (6th ed., pp. 775–812). Wiley.

Inman, A. G., Hutman, H., Pendse, A., Devdas, L., Luu, L., & Ellis, M. V. (2014). Current trends concerning supervisors, supervisees, and clients in clinical supervision. In C. E. Watkins Jr. & D. Milne (Eds.), *Wiley international handbook of clinical supervision* (pp. 61–102). Wiley. https://doi.org/10.1002/978111884360

Morgan, M. M., & Sprenkle, D. H. (2007). Toward a common-factors approach to supervision. *Journal of Martial and Family Therapy, 13*, 1–17. https://doi.org/10.1111/j.1752-0606.2007.0001.x

Paige, S., & Wosket, V. (2015). *Supervising the counsellor and psychotherapist: A cyclical model* (3rd ed.). Routledge.

Passmore, G. J., Turner, A., & Prescott, J. (2019). *Identity structure analysis and teacher mentorship: Across the context of Shools and the individual*. Palgrave.

Watkins, E. C. (2017). How does psychotherapy supervision work? Contributions of connection, conception, allegiance, alignment and action. *Journal of Psychotherapy Integration., 27*(2), 201–217.

Watkins, C. E., Jr., Budge, S. L., & Callahan, J. L. (2015). Common and specific factors converging in psychotherapy supervision: A supervisory extrapolation of the Wampold/Budge psychotherapy relationship model. *Journal of Psychotherapy Integration, 25*, 214–235. https://doi.org/10.1037/a0039561

Watkins, C. E., Jr., & Scaturo, D. J. (2013). Toward an integrative, learning-based model of psychological interventions, and supervisee learning/relearning. *Journal of Psychotherapy Integration, 23*, 75–95. https://doi.org/10.1037/a0031330

Weinreich, P. (2003). Theory and practice: Introduction. In Weinreich & Saunderson (Eds.), *Analysing identity: Clinical, societal and cross-cultural contexts* (pp. 1–5). Taylor and Francis, Routledge, and Psychology Press.

Wheeler, S. (2003). *Research on supervision of counsellors and psychotherapists: A systematic scoping search.* BACP.

Wheeler, S., & Richards, K. (2007). The impact of clinical supervision on counselors and therapists, their practice and their clients: A systematic review of the literature. *Counselling & Psychotherapy Research, 7*, 54–65. https://doi.org/10.1080/14733140601185274

Wilson, H. M. N., Davies, J. A., & Weatherhead, S. (2016). Trainee therapists' experiences of supervision during training: A meta-synthesis. *Clinical Psychology & Psychotherapy, 23*, 340–351. https://doi.org/10.1002/CPP.1957

CHAPTER 2

# The Indeterminate Identity Variant

**Abstract** This chapter provides discussion on the importance of identity for professional development. Thereafter, the chapter provides an analysis of an ISA report, an example of indeterminate ISA identity variant. The analysis builds on our prior work (Passmore, Turner, & Prescott, Identity structure analysis and teacher mentorship: Across the context of schools and the individual. Palgrave, 2019) through the provision of tables taken from an Ipseus report. The tables and accompanying descriptive text serve to guide the reader in interpreting outputs from the Ipseus software. That is, the tables and text are designed to exemplify the template in action. They walk the reader through the process of using an Ipseus report for successful ISA analysis. Also described are our efforts at building upon the template to maximise the feedback that can be generated for counselling for PD. That is, the chapter describes our attempt to standardise the reporting of ISA parameters such as structural pressures and associated core and conflicted constructs according to the template description. This chapter also describes our approach to reporting patterns in raw scores. The use of patterns in raw scores in an ISA analysis adds considerably to the original descriptive power of the template in regard to the nature of idealistic, contra and conflicted identification.

**Keywords** Indeterminate identity variant • Raw scores • Identity • Identity theory • Social identity theory • Self-categorisation theory •

© The Author(s), under exclusive license to Springer Nature Switzerland AG 2022
G. Passmore, J. Prescott, *Using an ISA Mobile App for Professional Development*, https://doi.org/10.1007/978-3-030-99071-8_2

Professional development • Structural pressure • Core constructs • Conflicted constructs • Idealistic identifications • Contra identifications • Empathetic identification • Conflicted identification • Evaluation of others • Ego-involvement with others

## Introduction

Identity is a dynamic construct, with people having multiple identities. These identities will be salient at different times, depending on the role the individual is undertaking (Simpson & Carroll, 2008). Within the field of psychology, there are three main identity theories: identity theory, social identity theory and self-categorisation theory. Identity theorists argue that the core of identity is the categorisation of the self in particular roles and the meanings and expectations within those role(s) (Stets & Burke, 2000). A salient identity will determine the behavioural choices of an individual at a given time. Therefore, more time and energy are given to the salient roles and identities of individuals (Greenhaus & Powell, 2003). Social identity theorists suggest that individual identity is formed through the social roles and categories those individuals hold. These multiple roles and identities form the self (Ashforth & Mael, 1989). Self-categorisation theory, as proposed by Turner et al. (1987), suggests that individuals categorise themselves on a personal level (individual) and a group level (group membership). Therefore, behaviour is determined based on whether an individual is behaving according to an individual or a group-level membership. Work and our job role can represent an important social category to many individuals (Hogg & Terry, 2000). The more an individual identifies with an organisation or a profession, the more they will act in accordance with the group norms and values of that organisation or profession, resulting in stronger support for the organisation or profession (Hogg & Terry, 2000). Identification with a profession is a cognitive attitude towards that organisation or profession and this identification involves the individual incorporating the norms and values of the organisation/profession (Hogg & Terry, 2000). This identification occurs when an individual integrates their beliefs about that organisation or profession into their own identity. When this identification is strong in an individual, it becomes a part of their self-concept. This professional identification has strong links to intention to leave an organisation or profession and job satisfaction (Van Dick et al., 2004). An individual's level of identification is related to commitment, loyalty and motivation to the organisation or profession (Ashforth & Mael, 1989; Elsbach, 1999). How we identify with a profession is important and professional development is an important process in supporting individuals. In the text that follows, we consider the new ISA instrument developed for counselling supervision and why we feel that ISA can play an important role in counselling supervision.

## Professional Development and Clinical Supervision

Professional development in the form of clinical supervision involves a more experienced professional mentoring a less experienced professional. Clinical supervision has been defined as '*the provision of guidance of clinical practice for qualified health professionals by a more experienced health professional*' (Snowdon et al., 2017, p. 2). Many professions involve supervision for professional development with research finding that regular clinical supervision is linked with greater wellbeing in nurses (Oates, 2018); it has also been found to allow clinical staff to debrief and make sense of workplace complexities (Jarden et al., 2019; Brennan, 2017). Regular, high-quality supervisions have been found to be efficacious to monitor and reduce stress and burnout in clinical settings (Love et al., 2017; Johnson et al., 2020).

## The Self-Summary

When working on any ISA analysis (with any instrument, not just the Counselling supervision instrument), the first step should be to briefly consider the self-summary on page 4 of the Ipseus, ISA report. Doing so provides the analyst with an overview of the nature of the identity under consideration, be it foreclosed, of high or low self-evaluation, or indeed in crisis.

In Fig. 2.1, three of the entities of self (represented by the red circles) lie in the desired indeterminate (middle) identity variant section. One way to look at ISA analysis is to say that its goals are to lay bare explanations for deviations of the entities of self from the desired, central indeterminate section (see Fig. 2.2). For the purposes of this book, the reasons for the deviations will be assumed to lie primarily with the conflicted constructs, the contra identifications, and the idealistic identifications at play. That is, we will use examinations of raw scores associated with these ISA parameters to uncover the nature of deviations of entities of self from the

**Fig. 2.1** Representation of the ISA identity variants of the identity of Chap. 2

indeterminate identity variant. This is the analytical tack we took in the past in Passmore et al. (2019). In the remaining chapters of this book, we will expand on our description of this analytical approach to include images of patterns in the raw scores associated with these ISA parameters. In so doing, we will build upon the description of ISA analysis in Passmore et al. (2019) and better reveal our reasoning regarding the deviation of entities of self from the desired indeterminate rating.

Note, page 4 of the Ipseus report places entities of self in a chart of self-evaluation vs diffusion. Diffusion in ISA references the magnitude and dispersion of conflicted identifications to the extent that conflicted identifications represent diffusion; the horizontal axis of Fig. 2.2 is

| Defensive High Self-Regard | Confident | Diffuse High Self-Regard |
|---|---|---|
| Defensive | Indeterminate | Diffusion |
| Defensive Negative | Negative | Crisis |

**Fig. 2.2** Demarcation of identity variants

representative of the stages of Marcia's Identity Status theory. In ISA too, self-evaluation is similar to, but not the same as, self-esteem. Page 4 of the Ipseus report provides a table that demarcates ratings of entities of self according to their intersecting self-evaluation and diffusion values, as shown in Fig. 2.2.

In ISA, groupings of entities of self within a section of Fig. 2.2 are said to represent particular identity variants. For example, where entities of self appear to the left of the horizontal axis for the most part, a defensive identity is said to be at play. Where the grouping of entities of self appears toward the left of the horizontal axis in combination with high self-evaluation (the top left square of Fig. 2.2), a foreclosed identity is represented. A grouping of entities of self in the lower right square of Fig. 2.2 represents an identity in crisis (low self-evaluation and high-level diffusion). The identity associated with Fig. 2.1 is largely indeterminate. Once again, beginning an ISA analysis with a review of page 4 of the Ipseus report is useful as it quickly informs the researcher about the overall nature of an identity.

Our focus on the counselling supervision instrument permits, we feel, the creation of advisements for PD. We will use the terms counselling supervision or PD interchangeably as we work through our analyses in this study. The analytical approach we describe can be applied to the analysis of any identity for any ISA instrument.

## Structural Pressure

The second analytical step is to go to page 19 of the ISA report where parameter ranges are recorded (see Fig. 2.3 below).

To save shifting between page 19 and pages 12 and 13 (and indeed other pages of the Ipseus report) when working on an analysis for structural pressure, it is useful to print page 19 or make a note of the ranges (low and high cut off values) for pressured, core, secondary, conflicted and contradictory constructs on a sheet of paper. On the same note, write down the ranges for emotional significance, idealistic, contra, conflicted identification, self-evaluation and so on. Doing so will facilitate ready identification of core and conflicted constructs and provide ready access to other significant ISA parameter values as the remaining pages of the Ipseus report are referenced.

| Parameter | Sub-range | Mean | StD | Min | Low | High | Max |
|---|---|---|---|---|---|---|---|
| **Identity Variant:** | | | | | | | |
| Self Evaluation | | 0.12 | 0.58 | -1.00 | -0.46 | 0.69 | 1.00 |
| Identity Diffusion | | 0.39 | 0.24 | 0.00 | 0.15 | 0.63 | 1.00 |
| **Entity:** | | | | | | | |
| Ego-Involvement | | 3.04 | 0.94 | 0.00 | 2.10 | 3.98 | 5.00 |
| Evaluation | | -0.03 | 0.57 | -1.00 | -0.39 | 0.54 | 1.00 |
| | High | | | | 0.59 | | 1.00 |
| | Moderate | | | | 0.54 | | 0.59 |
| | Low | | | | -0.54 | | 0.54 |
| | Negative | | | | -1.00 | | -0.54 |
| Splits | | 0.58 | 0.32 | 0.00 | 0.26 | 0.90 | 1.00 |
| **Construct:** | | | | | | | |
| Emotional Significance | | 8.04 | 1.63 | 0.00 | 6.41 | 9.66 | 10.00 |
| Structural Pressure | | 72.58 | 21.39 | -100.00 | 51.19 | 93.96 | 100.00 |
| | Pressured | | | | 94.65 | | 100.00 |
| | Core | | | | 77.92 | | 94.65 |
| | Secondary | | | | 56.54 | | 77.92 |
| | Conflicted | | | | -56.54 | | 56.54 |
| | Contradictory | | | | -100.00 | | -56.54 |
| **Identification:** | | | | | | | |
| Idealistic | | 0.39 | 0.40 | 0.00 | 0.00 | 0.80 | 1.00 |
| Contra | | 0.53 | 0.41 | 0.00 | 0.12 | 0.94 | 1.00 |
| Empathetic | | 0.44 | 0.33 | 0.00 | 0.11 | 0.77 | 1.00 |
| Conflicted | | 0.32 | 0.28 | 0.00 | 0.03 | 0.60 | 1.00 |

**Fig. 2.3** ISA parameter ranges for the identity of Chap. 2

Begin the analysis of core and conflicted constructs by stating the nature of Structural Pressure and Emotional Significance and by stating their absolute ranges (the min and max values provided on page 19 of the Ipseus report). Note that the analysis of all parameters of the template begins with the presentation of a statement of definition.

### Structural Pressure and Emotional Significance

*Emotional Significance: Minimum value = 0.00, maximum value = 100.00*

The emotional significance of a construct used in the appraisal of the counsellors' social world is defined as the strength of affect associated with the expression of the construct. The index of standardised emotional significance can range from 0.00 (no significance) to 10.00 (maximal significance).

*Structural Pressure: Minimum value = -100, maximum value = +100*

Structural Pressure reflects the consistency with which a construct is used to evaluate entities. High Structural Pressure constructs are used in a consistent manner to evaluate others. They represent the core, stable evaluative dimensions of the identity under consideration. Low Structural Pressure constructs are used to evaluate others in different ways depending on circumstance and context. Low Structural Pressure suggests an area of stress and indecision; a conflicted dimension liable to poor decision making.

Page 12 of the Ipseus report (see Fig. 2.4 below) reveals which constructs are core or conflicted (high and low respectively). Page 13 (see Fig. 2.5 below) reveals the structural pressure and emotional significance values associated with the constructs of the instrument for the identity of concern.

Locate the core and conflicted constructs using the vertical hi and lo marker lines on page 12 and enter their left and right-side names appropriately into the Pole 1 and Pole 2 columns of a table (see Table 2.1 below). Continue onto page 13 which gives numeric values for the structural pressure and the emotional significance of the constructs. Enter the values into the table (see Table 2.1) as indicated below. Note that to guide the reader of a report, the positively (red) ascribed pole should be entered into Table 2.1 using italics.

To complete a report on SP findings, generate text beneath the table in step-wise fashion as follows:

# 38   G. PASSMORE AND J. PRESCOTT

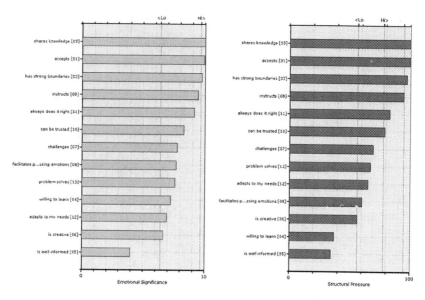

**Fig. 2.4**   Constructs of low and high SP

| | | # | Polarity | Emotional Significance | Structural Pressure | +ve Component | -ve Component | |
|---|---|---|---|---|---|---|---|---|
| accepts | < | 01 | -1 | 9.95 | 99.48 | 99.48 | 0.00 | judges |
| has strong boundaries | < | 02 | -1 | 9.73 | 97.33 | 97.33 | 0.00 | struggles to keep boundaries |
| shares knowledge | < | 03 | -1 | 10.00 | 100.00 | 100.00 | 0.00 | doesn't share knowledge |
| willing to learn | < | 04 | -1 | 7.26 | 37.10 | 54.87 | 17.77 | closed to learning |
| is well informed | < | 05 | -1 | 3.96 | 34.43 | 37.01 | 2.59 | is poorly informed |
| is creative | < | 06 | -1 | 6.66 | 56.43 | 61.52 | 5.09 | sticks to the tried and tested |
| challenges | < | 07 | -1 | 7.77 | 69.46 | 73.60 | 4.14 | never challenges |
| instructs | < | 08 | -1 | 9.46 | 94.56 | 94.56 | 0.00 | encourages reflection |
| facilitates processing emotions | < | 09 | -1 | 7.70 | 60.22 | 68.59 | 8.37 | leads to hiding emotions |
| can be trusted | < | 10 | -1 | 8.31 | 78.95 | 81.02 | 2.07 | cannot be trusted |
| always does it right | < | 11 | -1 | 9.15 | 83.18 | 87.32 | 4.14 | makes mistakes |
| adapts to my needs | < | 12 | -1 | 6.94 | 65.23 | 67.30 | 2.07 | is quite rigid in approach |
| problem solves | < | 13 | -1 | 7.99 | 67.13 | 71.53 | 4.40 | worries or avoids |

**Fig. 2.5**   Construct detail

**Table 2.1**  Core and conflicted values and beliefs

| Pole 1 | Pole 2 | Structural Pressure | Emotional Significance |
|---|---|---|---|
| **Core constructs** | | | |
| shares knowledge | doesn't share knowledge | 100.00 | 10.00 |
| accepts | judges | 99.48 | 9.95 |
| has strong boundaries | struggles to keep boundaries | 97.33 | 9.73 |
| instructs | encourages reflection | 94.56 | 9.46 |
| always does it right | makes mistakes | 83.18 | 9.15 |
| can be trusted | cannot be trusted | 78.95 | 8.31 |
| **Conflicted Constructs** | | | |
| is creative | sticks to the tried and tested | 56.43 | 6.66 |
| is willing to learn | is closed to learning | 37.10 | 7.26 |
| is well informed | is poorly informed | 34.43 | 3.96 |

1. list the core constructs.
2. note the themes the core constructs fall into.
   1. Doing so will reveal which, if any, theme or themes is/are dominant regarding an identity which in and of itself may be revelatory.
   2. If need be, make a note as to the distribution of core constructs across the themes. Sometimes core constructs are distributed evenly across the themes of an instrument.
3. Use the ranges jotted down from page 19 to identify which constructs are pressured and which are core.
4. Use the ranges to also determine which of the pressured and core constructs are of high and low emotional significance.

Regarding the interpretation of Table 2.1, note that pressured constructs of high emotional significance represent pivotal black and white issues for the identity in question. Indicate also that core and pressured constructs represent arenas where behaviour can be expected to conform to favoured poles for the most part. Make a note if necessary that in the case of secondary constructs, values and beliefs and any behaviours associated with the favoured pole are likely to be less reliably expressed than the values and beliefs and the behaviours of core constructs.

If one theme dominates note that a potential area of focus for counselling supervision may be to hand. Where the emotional significance of a pressured or core construct is high, the client is likely aware of the influence it holds over them. Nonetheless, it is the case that the participant will not likely welcome direct counselling to better engage with the construct as they will feel sure of their stance toward it. Where emotional significance is moderate or low, a supervisee may not be aware of the influence of a construct and as such, supervision toward it may be resisted as it is not on the supervisee's radar. Where constructs have low structural pressure (conflicted) and high emotional significance, a client will likely be aware of issues that surround them. Attempts to improve behaviours associated with the latter constructs will likely receive a warm reception.

In regard to conflicted constructs, use the ranges to confirm that the low-rated constructs of page 12 are truly conflicted. After listing the conflicted constructs beneath Table 2.1, consider their associated themes and their emotional significance. Finding a dominant theme for the conflicted constructs is considered useful for its potential to denote an area of focus for counselling supervision.

When an ISA analyst is writing up an analysis for the purpose of counselling supervision for an individual in regard to conflicted constructs, it is important to tell the counselor to explore the constructs with the supervisee. That is, make note that the supervisor should ask the supervisee to volunteer information regarding where and how the constructs have proved to be of difficulty in the past. With this information at hand, the supervisor can then draw plans up with the supervisee for reaching a firmer position with respect to the conflicted constructs. Future supervision sessions can work to improve (values and beliefs) behaviours around the constructs as a result of the client's implementation of the plans.

In addition to the above, ISA recommends an indirect approach to counselling supervision regarding pressured and core constructs. This tack involves asking the supervisee a question that associates a conflicted construct with one that is pressured or core. That is, ask the supervisor to think of a question that can be posed that brings the two constructs of note into play. For the supervisee under consideration, a suitable question might be 'in what ways might being poorly informed influence the need to share knowledge?' Below we indicate how the text created for PD around core and conflicted constructs might look for the identity represented in Table 2.1.

The core constructs of the supervisee of this chapter are: shares knowledge, accepts has strong boundaries, instructs, always does it right, can be trusted. The first 3 of these listed constructs are pressured and they are of high emotional significance. Pressured constructs are seen in ISA as pivotal, black and white issues for the identity in question. That they are emotionally significant suggests that in this case, the client is likely aware of the influence they hold over the identity. The fourth listed construct (instructs) is very much on the borderline of core and pressured. Shares knowledge lies in the formative theme of the instrument. Accepts and has strong boundaries respectively lie in the restorative and normative themes. The remaining core constructs (instructs, always does it right, and can be trusted) are constructs of the normative theme. The normative theme is the dominant theme in terms of the number of core constructs (4) at play. The remaining themes hold one pressured construct each. The pressured constructs are of high emotional significance as is the construct 'instructs'. The remaining core constructs are of moderate emotional significance. The preponderance of pressured constructs of high-level emotional significance is interesting and suggests that suitable targets for supervision will turn up as the analysis progresses to consideration of conflicted constructs.

The conflicted constructs of concern are: is creative, is willing to learn, and, is well informed. Of these constructs, the latter two reside in the formative theme of the instrument. Being creative or sticking to the tried and true is a construct of the normative theme. The first two of the listed conflicted constructs are of moderate emotional significance while 'is well informed' is of low emotional significance. It may or may not be the case that the identity under investigation is aware that these constructs represent problem arenas.

Supervising toward conflicted constructs is the preferred tack in ISA as it is here that a person is unsure of his/her thinking. Such counselling supervision will fare best if it focuses on conflicted constructs where the subject is aware (emotionally significant conflicted constructs) that a problem exists. Given the moderate to low emotional significance of the conflicted constructs at play, the supervisor has to chance that there is awareness of one or more of them. These caveats aside, counselling supervision might begin by introducing questions that aim to uncover the nature of the issues around the conflicted constructs. A suitable opening question might be, can you think of situations where you have struggled over whether it is better to stick to the tried and true or be creative?

Should information be forthcoming, develop plans for reaching firmer ground regarding this construct. Subsequent supervision would work to firm up understanding of how to act regarding this construct. The same tack would be applied for the remaining conflicted constructs, which by the way are subject to structural pressure that sees them classified as contradictory in nature.

To associate a conflicted construct with a core or pressured construct, a first line of questioning could concern: the pressured construct shares knowledge/doesn't share knowledge and the conflicted construct is well-informed/is poorly informed. For example, are there times when keeping knowledge back might be better regarding the degree to which a person is informed?

## Idealistic and Contra Identifications

Here we shift from the consideration of constructs to the consideration of identification patterns.

Start this section of the report by stating the ranges and definitions of the parameters:

*Idealistic Identification: minimum value = 0.00, maximum value = 1.00*
*Contra-Identification: minimum value = 0.00, maximum value = 1.00*

*Idealistic identifications (II) point to a person's role models. They indicate the characteristics a person will seek to emulate over the long term.*

*Contra-identifications (CI) indicate negative role models. Those who possess characteristics from which a person wishes to dissociate.*

Then turn to page 14 of the Ipseus report and enter into a table (Table 2.2) the significant and borderline significant entities of idealistic and contra-identification for the identity in question. Begin the analysis beneath the table by listing the entities associated with significant (and where it is considered necessary, borderline significant) idealistic and contra identification (the ranges from page 19 of the Ipseus report will be needed for this step). For the identity under review, this text might appear as:

This identity exhibits strong positive identification with 'a professional I admire' and 'a good friend'.

2 THE INDETERMINATE IDENTITY VARIANT    43

**Table 2.2** Idealistic and contra identifications

| Entity | Ideal | Contra |
|---|---|---|
| A professional I admire | 1.00 | |
| A good friend | 0.92 | |
| A professional I don't admire | | 1.00 |
| A public figure I don't admire | | 0.92 |
| Key adult female | | 0.92 |

Next, turn to writing up an analysis around the raw scores that were calculated by Ipseus along a -4 to +4, 9-point scale from the ratings (1–9) entered into Ipseus, or in the case of this book, into the app. Note that Ipseus determines the -4 to +4 raw scores from the 1 through 9 ratings by anchoring against the universally admired entity (me as I would like to be, for example) of the instrument. That is, the pole of each construct that a study's participant associates with 'me as I would like to be' is accorded a positive score.

Raw scores help facilitate the creation of counselling advice and they facilitate the generation of explanations for the deviation of entities of self from the central 'indeterminate' section of Fig. 2.2. In ISA, the description of idealistic identification suggests that the examination of raw scores should focus on how the entity of interest (an entity of current self) compares to the ideal self (me as I would like to be). However, it may be that life circumstances involving the issue associated with the instrument can, and perhaps will, prohibit behaving as per the client(s) ideal self. In such a case, it might be better to compare the raw scores of the target entity of the current self to another entity of idealistic identification. Deciding which entities to focus upon when using raw scores is a matter of judgement based in the entities of the instrument to hand, the nature (the issue to hand) of the instrument, and the interests of the supervisor.

To report raw scores for idealistic identification, simply go to page 18 (Fig. 2.6) of the Ipseus report and note those constructs where the first selected entity of idealistic identification (me as I would like to be) scores more toward the favoured pole than the second target entity of current self (me as a professional in this case). These raw scores represent areas of long-term behavioural aspiration and as such they should be targets of counselling supervision. An examination of raw scores for the identity under investigation points to: accepts, has strong boundaries instructs, is willing to learn, challenges, is well informed, and is creative, as the poles of the constructs where 'me as a professional' compares unfavourably to me as I would like to be.' Note that accepts and boundaries are pivotal and

|  | C# | 01 | 02 | 03 | 04 | 05 | 06 | 07 | 08 | 09 | 10 | 11 | 12 | 13 | |
|---|---|---|---|---|---|---|---|---|---|---|---|---|---|---|---|
| accepts | 01 | 4 | -4 | 1 | 2 | 4 | 3 | -3 | -2 | -4 | -1 | 3 | 2 | -4 | judges |
| has strong boundaries | 02 | 4 | -4 | 1 | 2 | 3 | 3 | -3 | -2 | -4 | -2 | 2 | 2 | -4 | struggles to keep boundaries |
| shares knowledge | 03 | 3 | -4 | 0 | 2 | 3 | 3 | -4 | -1 | -4 | -4 | 3 | 1 | -3 | doesn't share knowledge |
| willing to learn | 04 | 1 | -4 | 2 | -1 | -1 | 2 | -2 | 0 | 4 | -2 | 2 | 3 | -2 | closed to learning |
| is well informed | 05 | 2 | 2 | 1 | 0 | -1 | 2 | -1 | -1 | -2 | 0 | 3 | 3 | 0 | is poorly informed |
| is creative | 06 | 2 | -4 | -2 | 2 | 1 | 2 | -3 | -1 | -2 | -2 | -1 | 3 | -2 | sticks to the tried and tested |
| challenges | 07 | 2 | -4 | 1 | 1 | 3 | 2 | -4 | -1 | -1 | -2 | 2 | 3 | 2 | never challenges |
| instructs | 08 | 4 | -4 | 1 | 2 | 4 | 1 | -4 | -2 | -4 | -2 | 2 | 4 | 2 | encourages reflection |
| facilitates processing emotions | 09 | 1 | -4 | -1 | -1 | -2 | 3 | -2 | -2 | -4 | -2 | 2 | 2 | -2 | leads to hiding emotions |
| can be trusted | 10 | 2 | -4 | 3 | 2 | 2 | 2 | -4 | -2 | -4 | -3 | 2 | 1 | 1 | cannot be trusted |
| always does it right | 11 | 2 | -4 | 2 | 2 | 2 | 2 | -4 | -1 | -4 | -4 | 1 | 3 | 2 | makes mistakes |
| adapts to my needs | 12 | 2 | -4 | 2 | 2 | 1 | 2 | -4 | 0 | -1 | -4 | 0 | 2 | 1 | is quite rigid in approach |
| problem solves | 13 | 3 | -4 | -1 | 0 | 3 | 2 | -4 | 2 | -1 | -2 | 2 | 2 | -1 | worries or avoids |

Fig. 2.6 Raw scores

pressured constructs and that instructs is borderline pressured. Note also that willing to learn, is well informed, and is creative are conflicted constructs for this identity. Where an entity of self deviates from the indeterminate rating, counselling to uncover factors in the workplace that are preventing or inhibiting the desired behaviour in regard to the noted constructs (long-term behavioural aspirations) is recommended. When circumstances dictate that a comparison of 'me as a professional' to other entities of idealistic identification is required, and where the same constructs are at issue across such comparisons, we suggest that the need to counsel toward those positive aspirational behaviours is reinforced.

Turning to the contra-identification pattern we see that a professional I don't admire, a public figure I don't admire and key adult female are the entities of note. In the case of a professional I don't admire the degree of contra-identification is significant. Contra-identification for the remaining entities is borderline high. A comparison of 'me as a professional' to 'a professional I don't admire' ought to turn up behaviours the identity wishes to shun in the workplace. The latter entity is perceived to exhibit behaviours along the negatively rated poles of all of the constructs of the instrument. Rather than engaging in a consideration of all of the constructs of the instrument, we suggest in cases like this that the analysis focus upon those constructs where comparison is most unfavourable. In regard to the identity of this chapter, this might appear as: judges, struggles to keep boundaries, doesn't share knowledge, cannot be trusted, makes mistakes, and, is quite rigid in approach. That a professional I don't admire is seen to behave opposite to the client's preferred behaviours along 3 pressured constructs (judges, doesn't share knowledge, struggles to keep boundaries) reveals much about the source of the contra-identification. As per idealistic identification, we suggest that different entities can be used for the purposes of comparison at the discretion of the analyst.

## Empathetic Identification

This parameter is reported on page 15 of the Ipseus report. Begin as before by describing its nature and its range.

*Empathetic Identification: minimum value = 0.00, maximum value = 1.00 Whereas idealistic identifications represent long-term aspirations; empathetic identifications are of the here and now. Change in empathetic identifications across context and mood states reflects potential for change in behaviour.*

Then list the significant empathetic identifications on display. Figure 2.7 is taken from page 15 of the Ipseus report.

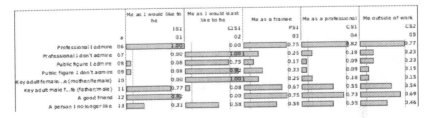

**Fig. 2.7** Empathetic identification pattern

Current empathetic identifications based in 'me as a professional' are with a professional I admire (0.82), a good friend (0.73)
Current empathetic identifications based in 'me outside of work' are with a professional I admire (0.77), a good friend (0.69)
Past empathetic identification based in 'me as a trainee' are with a professional I admire (0.75), a good friend (0.75)

With the entities of note so listed, the analysis turns to generating text that describes any changes in the degree of empathetic identification across context, mood states or time. Such changes are said to reflect the potential for change in behaviour as the identity shifts between the domains of the instrument. That is, while idealistic and contra-identification patterns point to long-term behavioural goals, empathetic findings concern the potential for behaviours the client is likely to engage in in the here and now. The findings derived from Fig. 2.7 might generate the following text.

The quantitative values extracted from Fig. 2.7 point to an identity that exhibits a similar pattern of empathetic identification across the domains of work and outside work and across the entity of current self (me as a professional) and the entity of past self (me as a trainee). In regard to empathetic identification then, the supervisee is quite stable. It is encouraging that the identity feels it behaves most like the entities of empathetic identification in the context of me as a professional, the entities involved are also entities of idealistic identification.

## CONFLICTED IDENTIFICATION

Turning to page 16 of the report we find a table that presents the findings for conflicted identification. Begin with a description and range as per all prior ISA parameters:

*Conflicted Identification: minimum value = 0.00, maximum value = 1.00*
*Conflicted Identification in ISA references the combination of contra- and empathetic identification with significant others; being 'as' another while at the same time wishing to disassociate from those characteristics that are seen to be held in common* (Fig. 2.8).

2 THE INDETERMINATE IDENTITY VARIANT    47

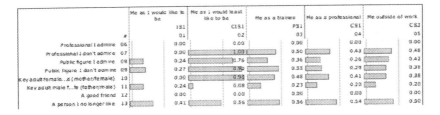

**Fig. 2.8** Conflicted identification pattern

Present the entities of significant conflicted identification:

Current conflicted identification based in 'me as a professional' are with a person I no longer like (0.54), a professional I don't admire (0.43)
Current conflicted identification based in 'me outside of work' are with a person I no longer like (0.50), a professional I don't admire (0.48)
Past conflicted identification based in 'me as a trainee' are with a person I no longer like (56), A public figure I don't admire (0.55), a professional I don't admire (0.50), key adult female (0.48)

The first step in developing counselling supervision advice using conflicted identification is to note whether the cause is due to idealistic or contra-identification (the extent to which these patterns of identification are high for the entities of conflicted identification). A conflict that is based in contra-identification (an entity of conflicted identification that is also an entity of contra-identification) likely warrants attention. Where a conflicted identification is based in idealistic identification, the positive nature of the finding suggests that the matter does not require supervision. It is the case that none of the conflicted identifications of this supervisee are significantly high, and as such none of them require counselling.

Where there is a need to shed light on conflicted identifications that are deemed worthy of supervision, we once again turn to raw scores. In Chap. 3, we present our approach to identifying constructs of conflicted identification in full. Here, given there are no entities of significant conflicted identification, we will describe the approach summarily. To begin, look for *negatively* scored constructs that the target entity (me as a professional in this case) and the entity(ies) of conflicted identification *have in common*. In other words, work to locate the constructs that have negative raw scores for both of the entities at play. Having identified such constructs, note if any of them are conflicted, core or pressured. This information can then be used to guide the creation of supervision advice that, if applied, may reduce the impact of conflicted identification(s).

Although there are no significant conflicted identifications at play for this identity, we will, for the purposes of illustration, exemplify the above reasoning. The negatively scored constructs associated with me as a professional are: is closed to learning, and, leads to hiding emotions. These constructs are also scored negatively for a professional I don't admire. These are the constructs we would suggest targeting where there a need to help overcome a conflicted identification.

## Evaluation of and Ego Involvement with Others

Turn to page 9 of the Ipseus report and present normal ranges and a description of the parameters at issue.

*Evaluation minimum value = -1.00 maximum value = +1.00*
*Ego-involvement minimum value = 0.00 maximum value = 5.00*
*Evaluation of others refers to a summation of the positive and negative scores associated with each entity. Entities as a result can have a positive or negative value for this parameter.*
*Ego involvement refers to the overall responsiveness to an entity in terms of the extensiveness in quantity (number of characteristics possessed) and strength (where the rating of each characteristic lies along the zero-center scale) of the attributes they are rated as possessing.*

Next, provide evaluation and ego-involvement ratings for the entities of primary investigative interest for the identity in question.

## Entities of Primary Investigative Interest

A professional I don't admire (evaluation of -0.81) (ego involvement: 4.38)
A person I no longer like (evaluation of -0.27) (ego involvement: 2.50)
A public figure I admire (evaluation of -0.60) (ego: 4.06)
A good friend (evaluation of 0.54) (ego: 2.71)

To complete this section of the analysis, select those entities that are mentioned repeatedly or markedly in the prior analyses of ISA parameters. Next, enter evaluation and ego involvement values for the entities you select as per the text immediately above. Note which of the entities are rated high or low and whether these findings are in accordance with the findings for ideal and contra identification. For example:

In the case of the supervisee of this chapter, a good friend is evaluated positively and the remaining entities of interest are evaluated negatively. This is in keeping with the idealistic and contra-identification patterns, as reported earlier in this analysis. The identity for the most part exhibits higher ego involvement with the negatively evaluated entities than with the positively evaluated entity. This suggests a greater desire to avoid engaging in the behaviours associated with the negatively rated entities than to mimic the behaviours of the positively evaluated entity.

## EVALUATION OF SELF, EXTENT OF IDENTITY DIFFUSION AND IDENTITY VARIANT

Begin by stating normal ranges and descriptions:

*Self-Evaluation: minimum value = -1.00, maximum value = 1.00.*
*Identity Diffusion: minimum value = 0.00, maximum value = 1.00.*
*Self-evaluation refers to measurements wherein characteristics associated with the various entities of self (me as a student teacher, me at work etcetera) are compared to characteristics associated with the ideal aspirational self (me as I would like to be).*
*Identity diffusion in ISA is a measure of the extent of a person's conflicts of identification.*

Next up, provide the following information from the self-tabulation of page 6 of the Ipseus report.

**'Me as I would like to be'**
Self-evaluation: 0.62
Identity diffusion: 0.12
Identity variant: Defensive
**'Me as I would least like to be'**
Self-evaluation: -1.0
Identity diffusion: 0.83
Identity Variant: Crisis
**Me, as trainee'**
Self-evaluation: 0.19
Identity diffusion: 0.38
Identity variant: Indeterminate

***'Me, as a professional***
Self –evaluation: 0.36
Identity Diffusion: 0.30
Identity Variant: Indeterminate
***'Me, outside of work***
Self –evaluation: 0.42
Identity Diffusion: 0.32
Identity Variant: Indeterminate

To complete the provision of information for this section of the analysis, return to page 4 of the Ipseus report and Fig. 2.1 of this analysis. Note please that in reporting an analysis, it is better to add Fig. 2.1 immediately above the information from the self-tabulation of page 6 rather than at the start of an analysis as we did for illustrative purposes at the start of this chapter. Doing so better illustrates for the reader how findings are derived from the diffusion and self-evaluation data. We adopt the latter tack in the remaining chapters of this text.

Begin the analysis of the information of page 4 begin by repeating what is evident in Fig. 2.1 (which entities of self are indeterminate and which are in crisis etc.). Add self-evaluation and identity diffusion values for the entities of self. Thereafter, turn the analysis toward unpacking the extent to which the ideal, contra, and, conflicted identification findings might shed light on any deviation of the entities of self from the indeterminate component of the table. It is the case that for the client under consideration, most of the entities of self are indeterminate in nature. Analysis would therefore focus on 'me as I would like to be' and 'me as I would least like to be'.

The most notable finding here is that 'me as I would least like to be' is in crisis. To counsel in regard to this finding helps the identity to rationalise their behaviour when they act out of character such that feeling better about their behaviour becomes a possibility.

It is encouraging that 'me as I would like to be', though presenting as a defensive entity of self, exhibits greater self-evaluation than 'me as a professional'. The suggestion is that the client holds out hope for improved future performance. Counselling supervision to help realise such improvement might focus on the relationship with entities of moderate conflicted identification such as 'a professional I don't admire'. This might involve helping the supervisee empathise with this entity by discussing reasons for the behaviours this entity is perceived to exhibit (behaviours made evident in the analyses of contra and conflicted identification). This approach to counselling supervision may work to improve any conflicted identification and shift this entity of self from the defensive variant toward an indeterminate rating.

## Summary of ISA Report

We noted in Chap. 1 that rather than the term 'holistic interpretation' that Weinreich suggested, we prefer to finish up an analytic report with 'summary of ISA report'. Creating the summary is a matter of reviewing the findings of the analysis and focusing in on the most useful findings. We present such a summary below for the identity we have considered in this chapter. It exemplifies the text that would be provided to guide a supervisor.

The core constructs of concern are: shares knowledge, instructs, accepts, always does it right, can be trusted and, facilitates processing emotions. The first 3 of these constructs are pressured and are of high emotional significance. Shares knowledge lies in the formative theme, accepts and facilitates processing emotions are restorative. The normative theme holds the core constructs: instructs, always does it right, and can be trusted. The latter is the dominant theme in terms of the number of core constructs. That said, only always does it right is pressured, the remaining constructs of this theme are core to the client and are associated with moderate emotional significance. Each of the remaining themes holds one pressured construct.

The conflicted constructs concern being: willing to learn, well informed and creative. Of these constructs, the first two reside in the formative theme of the instrument. Being creative or sticking to the tried and true is a construct of the normative theme, it is also the most conflicted construct. All of the conflicted constructs are of moderate emotional significance. It may or may not be the case that there is awareness that these constructs represent problem arenas.

Begin counselling supervision by introducing questions that aim to uncover the nature of issues around the conflicted constructs. For example, can you think of situations where you have struggled over whether it is better to stick to the tried and true or be creative? Use any information that is forthcoming to develop plans with the client for reaching firmer ground regarding this construct. Subsequent counselling supervision would work to firm up an understanding of how to act regarding this construct. Apply the same tack for the remaining conflicted constructs. To associate a conflicted construct with a core or pressured construct, consider asking: are there times when keeping knowledge back might be better regarding the degree to which a person is informed?

There is strong positive identification with 'a professional I admire' and 'a good friend'. Here the raw scores point to: accepts, has strong boundaries instructs, is willing to learn, challenges, is well informed, and is creative as the poles of the constructs where 'me as a professional' compares unfavourably to 'me as I would like to be'. Note that accepts and boundaries are pivotal and pressured constructs and that instructs is borderline pressured. Note also that willing to learn, is well informed and is creative are conflicted constructs for this identity. Counselling supervision to uncover factors in the workplace that are preventing the identity from behaving as desired in regard to the noted constructs (long-term behavioural aspirations) is recommended.

Regarding the contra-identification pattern, 'a professional I don't admire', 'a public figure I don't admire' and 'key adult female' are the entities of note. In the case of 'a professional I don't admire', the degree of contra-identification is significant. Contra-identification for the remaining entities is borderline high. A comparison of 'me as a professional' to 'a professional I don't admire' ought to turn up behaviours the identity wishes to shun in the workplace. The latter entity is perceived to exhibit behaviours along the negatively rated poles of all of the constructs of the instrument. The comparison is most unfavourable in regard to: judges, struggles to keep boundaries, doesn't share knowledge, cannot be trusted, makes mistakes, and, is quite rigid in approach. That a professional I don't admire is seen to behave opposite to the supervisee's preferred behaviours along 3 pressured constructs (judges, doesn't share knowledge, struggles to keep boundaries) reveals much about the source of the contra-identification.

The supervisee exhibits a similar pattern of empathetic identification across the domains of work and outside work and across the entity of current self (me as a professional) and the entity of past self (me as a trainee). It is encouraging that the entities of empathetic identification in the context of me as a professional are also entities of idealistic identification. There are no significant conflicted identifications at play for this identity.

A good friend is evaluated positively and the remaining entities of interest are evaluated negatively. This is in keeping with the idealistic and contra-identification patterns of this identity. For the most part, there is higher ego involvement with the negatively evaluated entities than with the positively evaluated entity. This suggests a greater desire to avoid engaging in the behaviours associated with the negatively rated entities than to mimic the behaviours of the positively evaluated entity.

Most of the entities of self-lie are indeterminate The most notable finding is that 'me as I would least like to be' is in crisis. To supervise in regard to this finding helps the identity to rationalise their behaviour when they act out of character such that feeling better about such behaviour becomes a possibility. It is encouraging that 'me as I would like to be', though presenting as a defensive entity of self, exhibits greater self-evaluation than 'me as a professional'. The finding suggests that the supervisee holds out hope for improved future performance. Supervision to help realise such improvement might focus on the client's relationship with entities of moderate conflicted identification such as 'a professional I don't admire'. That is, help the client empathise with this entity by discussing reasons for the perceived behaviours (behaviours made evident in the analyses of contra and conflicted identification for this entity). This approach to counselling supervision may work to improve the moderate conflicted identification and shift this entity of self from the defensive variant and toward an indeterminate rating.

## REFERENCES

Ashforth, B. E., & Mael, F. A. (1989). Social identity theory and the organization. *Academy of Management Review*, 14(1), 20–39.
Brennan, E. J. (2017). Towards resilience and wellbeing in nurses. *British Journal of Nursing*, 26(1), 43–47. https://doi.org/10.12968/bjon.2017.26.1.43
Elsbach, K. D. (1999). An expanded model of organizational identification. *Research in Organizational Behavior*, 21, 163–200.
Greenhaus, J. H., & Powell, G. N. (2003). When work and family collide: Deciding between competing role demands. *Organizational Behavior and Human Decision Processes*, 90, 291–303.
Hogg, M. A., & Terry, D. J. (2000). Social identity and self-categorization processes in organizational context. *Academy of Management Review*, 25, 121–140.
Jarden, R. J., Sandham, M., Siegert, R. J., & Koziol-McLain, J. (2019). Strengthening workplace well-being: Perceptions of intensive care nurses. *Nursing in Critical Care*, 24(1), 15–23. https://doi.org/10.1111/nicc.12386
Johnson, J., Corker, C., & O'connor, D. B. (2020). Burnout in psychological therapists: A cross-sectional study investigating the role of supervisory relationship quality. *Clinical Psychologist*, 24(3), 223–235. https://doi.org/10.1111/cp.12206

Love, B., Sidebotham, M., Fenwick, J., Harvey, S., & Fairbrother, G. (2017). "Unscrambling what's in your head": A mixed method evaluation of clinical supervision for midwives. *Women and Birth, 30*(4), 271–281. https://doi.org/10.1016/j.wombi.2016.11.002

Oates, J. (2018). What keeps nurses happy? Implications for workforce well-being strategies. *Nursing Management, 25*(1). https://doi.org/10.7748/nm.2018.e1643

Passmore, G. J., Turner, A., & Prescott, J. (2019). *Identity structure analysis and teacher mentorship: Across the context of shools and the individual.* Palgrave.

Simpson, B., & Carroll, B. (2008). Re-viewing 'role' in processes of identity construction. *Organization, 15*(1), 29–50.

Stets, J. E., & Burke, P.J. (2000). Identity theory and Social identity theory. *Social Psychology Quarterly, 63*(3), 224–237.

Snowdon, D. A., Leggat, S. G., & Taylor, N. F. (2017). Does clinical supervision of healthcare professionals improve effectiveness of care and patient experience? A systematic review. *BMC Health Services Research, 17*(1), 1–11. https://doi.org/10.1186/s12913-017-2739-5

Turner, J. C., Hogg, M. A., Oakes, P. J., Reicher, P. J., & Wetherall, M. S. (1987). *Rediscovering the social group: A self-categorization.* Blackwell.

Van Dick, R., Wagner, U., Stellmacher, J., & Christ, O. (2004). The utility of a broader conceptualization of organizational identification: Which aspects really matter? *Journal of Occupational and Organizational Psychology, 77*, 171–191.

CHAPTER 3

# The Defensive High Self Regard Identity Variant

**Abstract** This chapter presents theoretical data for the foreclosed identity variant. The aim of the chapter is to illustrate to the reader how this identity variant appears in an ISA, Ipseus report and how it can be analysed. To build on the reader's understanding of ISA analysis, this chapter includes figures and tables of raw scores taken from the report that Ipseus generated from the theoretical data. These figures and raw scores are provided to better the reader's understanding of how and why the interpretation of the raw scores might be useful in a professional development setting such as supervision or mentoring.

**Keywords** Defensive high self-regard identity variant • Identity status • Foreclosure • Identity diffusion • Moratorium • Achievement • Positive self-regard • Perceived self-competence • Fully functioning • Hypothetical data set

## INTRODUCTION

The previous chapters considered the development of an instrument, introduced the ISA method and touched upon its potential application in counselling supervision. The chapters also introduced the authors' ISA smartphone application and how to use it. To showcase the value of the

---

© The Author(s), under exclusive license to Springer Nature
Switzerland AG 2022
G. Passmore, J. Prescott, *Using an ISA Mobile App for Professional Development*, https://doi.org/10.1007/978-3-030-99071-8_3

ISA process for supervision—in this case, counselling supervision—this chapter (and later chapters) will consider in full how the reader (a supervisor) may interpret and use the raw data from an ISA report to ask questions in a counselling supervision session to support the professional development of the counsellor. This will enable the reader in understanding how they themselves may embed ISA within their supervision practice to help inform them of issues and help the supervisee understand themselves during the process. The questions suggested within the chapter may help the supervision process by allowing the opportunity to reflect on the analysis and interpretation of ISA reports as well as question and respond to the interpretations.

Identity foreclosure occurs when people think they know who they are but they have not yet fully explored options (Marcia, 1966). Identity development theorists posit that a foreclosed identity is one where an individual has committed to an identity without exploring alternatives and they have made a commitment too soon (Marcia, 1966). According to Marcia (1966), there are four identity statuses, based on the amount of exploration and commitment the individual has experienced. Identity diffusion indicates the individual has not yet made commitments regarding a specific developmental task, and may or may not have explored different developmental alternatives in that domain. Foreclosure means the individual has made a commitment without exploration. Within the moratorium stage, the individual is still exploring and has not yet committed, whereas the identity achievement stage shows an individual that has explored and committed to an identity.

To further introduce this chapter, we provide a brief account of what positive self-regard is within the counselling and the therapeutic setting. We also consider some literature around meaning of life and perceived self-competence. Positive self-regard reflects a person's contentedness with themselves in terms of their own standards (Leising et al., 2013). Personality constructs such as self-esteem, self-efficacy and depression reflect a person's evaluation of their self, with research finding high correlations between such constructs. Within therapy and the counselling setting, unconditional positive self-regard is regarded by humanistic psychologists as important to well-being. Carl Rogers (1961) viewed a fully functioning (now termed psychological well-being) person as someone open to experience, trusting of their own judgements, free to make choices and not governed by the values of others. Fully functioning has been viewed as someone who is authentic (Joseph, 2016), living according to their own intrinsic values/goals (Kasser & Ryan, 1993), and someone who is self-determining and not reliant on the views or values of others to guide their behavior (Ryan & Deci, 2000).

To introduce the defensive high self-regard of this chapter, we consider how work can differ for people in terms of its meaning and the value people give to it. Seligman (2004) suggests that people can view work in three distinct ways and that there is a difference between a job (work for money), a career (work for professional accomplishment) and a calling (working towards a greater good). With a calling being the most meaningful to individuals, providing a meaning in life (Coulson et al., 2013). Meaningful work is sought by many and has been linked to increased wellbeing (Edwards & Van Tongeren, 2020). Meaning in life has been found to buffer the effects of work stress (Harris et al., 2007) and burnout in hospice nurses (Barnett et al., 2019). The emotional support counsellors and therapists provide clients has been found to be a key source of meaning in life for counsellors (Cleary, 2019; Russo-Netzer et al., 2020). However, due to the emotional involvement counsellors invest in their work, counsellors are also at risk of burnout (Hardiman & Simmonds, 2013).

When considering high self-regard, we thought it would be interesting for the reader to mention perceived self-competence. Perceived self-confidence is the belief an individual has that they have the skill set for a certain career (Lippe et al., 2020). The ISA process can tease out the skills, or at least the confidence a person feels they have for a certain job, in this case study, the skills for being an effective counsellor. Perceived self-confidence differs from Bandura's self-efficacy theory, in that self-efficacy is domain specific and is the belief a person has in their ability to perform and behave in a certain role or domain and has been utilised a lot within career development theory (Bandura, 1977). Perceived self-confidence is more skill focused and is therefore useful to consider when looking at the use of ISA within supervision and the confidence individuals have in their skill set for the role. Perceived self-competence has been linked to increased meaning in life (Demirbaş-Çelik & Keklik, 2019). In a study looking at the meaning of life and the perceived competence of counselling students, Hurst and Prescott (2021) found higher levels of meaning of life correlated positively with the perceived competence scale, implying counselling to be a calling rather than a job.

## Creating Hypothetical Data Sets

Like Chap. 2, this and the remaining chapters of the book make use of hypothetical ISA data. Hypothetical data permits the exploration of identities that align to the 4 corners of the identity variant chart of page 4 of the Ipseus report (defensive high self-regard, diffuse high self-regard, crisis, and defensive negative). The chart and its identity variants are represented in Fig. 3.1. Exploring the identity variants permits the exploration of ISA's potential to contribute to PD efforts across the ISA identity spectrum.

Creating hypothetic data sets permits description of the structure of raw data of each identity variant. To explain, Ipseus normally anchors itself along the ratings provided for the typically positively rated entity. In the case of the counselling instrument, the entity me as I would like to be was created to be this entity. The entity 'me as I would least like to be' is (depending on the instrument this could be another ISA entity selected for its likely negative ratings) allotted negative ratings by Ipseus. The first task in creating a data set then is to enter values for these anchor entities (along different ends of the 9-point scale). Thereafter, entities of self (me at work, me in the past, me outside work etc.) can be accorded high (positive) or low (negative) evaluations by aligning them relative to the ratings of the positively and negatively rated entities of the instrument. Note that the same reasoning applies to the desired evaluation ranking of the remaining entities of the instrument.

| Defensive High Self-Regard | Confident | Diffuse High Self-Regard |
|---|---|---|
| Defensive | Indeterminate | Diffusion |
| Defensive Negative | Negative | Crisis |

**Fig. 3.1** Demarcation of identity variants

The above describes how entities of self are moved along the vertical axis of Fig. 3.1. Movement along the horizontal axis requires the creation of ratings that conform to our interpretation of the ISA parameter, conflicted identification. Recall that in Chap. 1, we said that conflicted identification reflects those negatively rated constructs that entities of self and other entities of an instrument have in common. A low number of negatively rated constructs across the entities results in alignment to the left of the horizontal axis of Fig. 3.1. Increasing the number of identification conflicts (more negatively rated constructs held in common) moves the entities of self to the right of the axis. Using this quite simple reasoning, we were able to generate hypothetical data sets in Microsoft XL. Entering the data into the mobile app provided Ipseus reports that presented as the desired identity variants.

Figure 3.2 presents the ratings that were entered into the mobile app and then ported into Ipseus to create the identity variant of this chapter. Figure 3.3 presents the raw data scores that Ipseus generated after anchoring (according to the positively and negatively rated entities) along the 9-point scale.

|  | ce | 01 | 02 | 03 | 04 | 05 | 06 | 07 | 08 | 09 | 10 | 11 | 12 | 13 |  |
|---|---|---|---|---|---|---|---|---|---|---|---|---|---|---|---|
| accepts | 01 | 1 | 3 | 1 | 1 | 1 | 1 | 9 | 1 | 3 | 2 | 3 | 1 | 1 | judges |
| has strong boundaries | 02 | 9 | 1 | 9 | 9 | 9 | 9 | 1 | 9 | 5 | 9 | 5 | 9 | 9 | struggles to keep boundaries |
| shares knowledge | 03 | 6 | 1 | 5 | 6 | 6 | 1 | 2 | 6 | 3 | 9 | 4 | 4 | 8 | doesn't share knowledge |
| willing to learn | 04 | 3 | 7 | 2 | 3 | 3 | 2 | 5 | 3 | 6 | 4 | 9 | 3 | 3 | closed to learning |
| is well informed | 05 | 1 | 6 | 1 | 1 | 3 | 1 | 6 | 1 | 4 | 1 | 9 | 3 | 4 | is poorly informed |
| is creative | 06 | 1 | 7 | 1 | 1 | 1 | 1 | 9 | 1 | 5 | 1 | 3 | 1 | 1 | sticks to the tried and tested |
| challenges | 07 | 7 | 3 | 5 | 7 | 6 | 7 | 2 | 8 | 1 | 8 | 5 | 9 | 4 | never challenges |
| instructs | 08 | 1 | 7 | 1 | 1 | 1 | 1 | 9 | 1 | 3 | 1 | 2 | 1 | 1 | encourages reflection |
| facilitates processing emotions | 09 | 9 | 3 | 7 | 8 | 6 | 7 | 1 | 7 | 3 | 9 | 5 | 8 | 3 | leads to hiding emotions |
| can be trusted | 10 | 1 | 6 | 1 | 1 | 2 | 1 | 5 | 2 | 6 | 1 | 2 | 2 | 6 | cannot be trusted |
| always does it right | 11 | 4 | 1 | 3 | 4 | 3 | 5 | 3 | 4 | 1 | 1 | 5 | 5 | 5 | makes mistakes |
| adapts to my needs | 12 | 1 | 3 | 1 | 1 | 1 | 1 | 8 | 1 | 3 | 1 | 3 | 1 | 1 | is quite rigid in approach |
| problem solves | 13 | 8 | 3 | 7 | 7 | 6 | 2 | 1 | 9 | 1 | 8 | 5 | 9 | 4 | worries or avoids |

**Fig. 3.2** Raw ratings

| | | Me as I would like to be | Me as I would least like to be | Me as a trainee | Me as a professional | Me outside of work | Professional I admire | Professional I don't admire | Public figure I admire | Public figure I don't admire | Key adult female...e (mother/female) | Key adult male f...le (father/male) | A good friend | A person I no longer like | |
|---|---|---|---|---|---|---|---|---|---|---|---|---|---|---|---|
| | | 00 | 01 | 02 | 03 | 04 | 05 | 06 | 07 | 08 | 09 | 10 | 11 | 12 | 13 | |
| accepts | 01 | 4 | 2 | 4 | 4 | 4 | 4 | -4 | 4 | 2 | 3 | | 4 | 4 | judges |
| has strong boundaries | 02 | 4 | -4 | 4 | 4 | 4 | 4 | -4 | 4 | | 4 | | 4 | 4 | struggles to keep boundaries |
| shares knowledge | 03 | 3 | -4 | | 1 | 3 | -4 | -3 | 1 | -2 | 4 | -1 | -1 | 3 | doesn't share knowledge |
| willing to learn | 04 | 2 | -2 | 3 | 2 | 3 | | 2 | 2 | -1 | 1 | -4 | 2 | 2 | closed to learning |
| is well informed | 05 | 4 | -1 | 4 | 4 | 2 | 4 | -1 | 4 | 1 | 4 | -4 | 2 | 1 | is poorly informed |
| is creative | 06 | 4 | -2 | 4 | 4 | 4 | 4 | -4 | 4 | 2 | 4 | 2 | 4 | 4 | sticks to the tried and tested |
| challenges | 07 | 2 | -2 | | 2 | 1 | 2 | -3 | 3 | -4 | 3 | | 4 | -1 | never challenges |
| instructs | 08 | 4 | -2 | 4 | 4 | 4 | 4 | -4 | 4 | 2 | 4 | 3 | 4 | 4 | encourages reflection |
| facilitates processing emotions | 09 | 4 | -3 | 2 | 3 | 1 | 2 | -4 | 2 | -2 | 4 | | 3 | -2 | leads to hiding emotions |
| can be trusted | 10 | 4 | -1 | 4 | 4 | 3 | 4 | | 3 | -1 | 4 | 3 | 3 | -1 | cannot be trusted |
| always does it right | 11 | 1 | 4 | 2 | 1 | 2 | | 2 | 1 | 4 | 4 | | 0 | | makes mistakes |
| adapts to my needs | 12 | 4 | 2 | 4 | 4 | 4 | -4 | 2 | 4 | 2 | 4 | 2 | 4 | 4 | is quite rigid in approach |
| problem solves | 13 | 3 | -2 | 2 | 2 | 1 | -3 | -4 | 4 | -4 | 3 | | 4 | -1 | worries or avoids |

Fig. 3.3 Raw scores

This chapter required entities of self that aligned to the left of the horizontal axis (low levels of conflicted identification) and toward the top of the vertical axis. Once again:

Movement toward the top of the vertical axis was accomplished by entering values for entities of self that were close to those of the entities me as I would like to be and opposite to those of me as I would least like to be.

Movement along the horizontal axis toward the left (low levels of identification conflict) were accomplished by entering values for non-entities of self that aligned to those of the entities of self.

This reasoning can be seen through a quick examination of the values in the columns and rows of Fig. 3.2. With this information at hand, counsellors ought to have a deeper understanding of the type of evaluations (ratings) clients make of others as they go about their daily lives.

Raw scores like those of Fig. 3.3 are used to interpret the ideal, contra and conflicted identification patterns in this and the remaining chapters of the book. Having described our approach to the creation of raw data sets, we can now move on to analyse the identity associated with the data set of Figs. 3.2 and 3.3.

## STRUCTURAL PRESSURE AND EMOTIONAL SIGNIFICANCE

*Emotional Significance: Minimum value = 0.00, maximum value = 100.00*
The emotional significance of a construct used in the appraisal of the supervises social world is defined as the strength of affect associated with the expression of the construct. The index of standardised emotional significance can range from 0.00 (no significance) to 10.00 (maximal significance).

*Structural Pressure: Minimum value = -100, maximum value = +100*
Structural Pressure reflects the consistency with which a construct is used to evaluate entities. High Structural Pressure constructs are used in a consistent manner to evaluate others. They represent the core, stable evaluative dimensions of the identity under consideration. Low Structural Pressure constructs are used to evaluate others in different ways depending on circumstance and context. Low Structural Pressure suggests an area of stress and indecision; a conflicted dimension liable to poor decision making (Table 3.1).

The core constructs of this identity concern: struggles to keep boundaries, is creative, instructs, adapts to my needs, accepts, can be trusted. The first 3 listed constructs are pressured. They are also emotionally

Table 3.1 Core and conflicted values and beliefs

| Pole 1 | Pole 2 | SP | ES |
|---|---|---|---|
| Core constructs | | | |
| has strong boundaries | *struggles to keep boundaries* | 97.24 | 9.72 |
| *is creative* | sticks to the tried and tested | 95.95 | 9.59 |
| *Instructs* | encourages reflection | 94.13 | 10.00 |
| *adapts to my needs* | is quite rigid in approach | 83.85 | 9.68 |
| *accepts* | Judges | 81.03 | 9.40 |
| *can be trusted* | cannot be trusted | 72.64 | 7.63 |
| Conflicted constructs | | | |
| *is willing to learn* | closed to learning | 43.34 | 5.23 |
| shares knowledge | *doesn't share knowledge* | 28.30 | 5.48 |
| *always does it right* | makes mistakes | 8.93 | 4.32 |

significant. The remaining constructs are of core structural pressure and, other than can be trusted, they are associated with high emotional significance. Pressured constructs are seen as pivotal and black and white issues for the identity in question. That these constructs are emotionally significant suggests that this foreclosed identity is aware of the influence they hold. This supervisee (hypothetical person) is likely to be aware of the influence of the core constructs (other than can be trusted) that are associated with high emotional significance. Four of the constructs lie in the normative theme of the instrument (struggles to keep boundaries, creative, instructs, can be trusted). Two of the constructs lie in the restorative theme (accepts and adapts to my needs).

The preponderance of core constructs in the normative theme implies that this is the predominant theme of the identity. Further, as this is the theme that holds the pressured constructs, it is likely that this theme can be usefully targeted in counselling supervision, that is, suitable targets for counselling supervision may turn up regarding this theme as the analysis progresses to consideration of conflicted constructs.

The conflicted constructs concern: willing to learn, doesn't share knowledge, always does it right. The conflicted constructs are not sufficiently stressed that they merit a contradictory ISA rating. They are associated with low (always does it right) to borderline-moderate, emotional significance so the identity in question may not be aware that they represent issues. Two of the conflicted constructs lie in the formative themes of the instrument. Always does it right is a normative construct. The weighting of conflicted formative constructs and the fact that no formative construct is core suggests that the client may struggle with this theme. However, before deciding to focus counselling supervision on the formative theme, there are 2 additional factors to consider. First, always does it right is the most stressed of the conflicted constructs. Second, no conflicted construct is of high-level emotional significance.

Counselling supervision toward conflicted constructs might begin by introducing questions that aim to uncover the nature of the issues around the most conflicted construct or constructs. A suitable opening question might therefore be 'can you talk about situations where you have struggled with the issue of making mistakes/always doing it right'. With notes taken from a discussion around this question, plans can be developed to reach firmer ground regarding the need to be right (or not). Subsequent supervision sessions could work to firm up the person's understanding of how to act regarding this construct. The same approach to questioning could be applied to the remaining conflicted constructs.

To associate a conflicted construct with a core or pressured construct, questioning could begin with the pressured construct, is creative/sticks to the tried and tested and the conflicted construct always does it right/ makes mistake. For example, how might being creative impact the notion of always being right versus making mistakes?

## IDEALISTIC AND CONTRA-IDENTIFICATIONS

*Idealistic Identification: minimum value = 0.00, maximum value = 1.00*
*Contra-Identification: minimum value = 0.00, maximum value = 1.00*
*Idealistic identifications (II) point to a person's role models. They indicate the characteristics a person will seek to emulate over the long term.*
*Contra-identifications (CI) indicate negative role models. Those who possess characteristics from which a person wishes to dissociate* (Table 3.2)

Idealistic identification is described as 'the similarity between the qualities one attributes to the other and those one would like to possess as part of one's ideal image' (Weinreich, 2003, p. 58). The identity of this chapter exhibits strong positive identification with a public figure I admire, and, key adult female. A good friend represents a borderline high idealistic identification. None of the entities of idealistic identification pertain directly to the workplace. Given our focus on professional development, we will work to uncover behaviours that the identity in question wishes to aspire toward over the long term in the workplace by comparing me as a professional to me as I would like to be. However, we note again that it is possible to interpret the idealistic identification parameter according to the circumstances of the analysis. We feel that this interpretation of idealistic identification is appropriate as it may be that an entity cannot

Table 3.2  Idealistic and contra-identifications

| Entity | II | CI |
| --- | --- | --- |
| A public figure I admire | 1.00 | |
| Key adult female (mother/care giver) | 1.00 | |
| A good friend | 0.85 | |
| A professional I don't admire | | 0.77 |

reasonably behave as desired (me as I would like to be) in the workplace. This being the case, a more practical comparison might involve me as a professional and a professional I admire. If an identity seeks public office, a comparison of me as a professional to a public figure I admire might be more productive. At the risk of repeating ourselves, in these comparisons, the analyst seeks to identify constructs where the raw scores of the admired entity scores are more positive than the workplace entity (Table 3.3).

In this comparison, the first thing to note is that me as a professional is not rated negatively in regard to a single construct. Further, it is only in regard to problem solves/worries or avoids that me as a professional is accorded a lower positive rating than me as I would like to be (and this is, a minor lower rating). This finding reflects the high ratings of entities of self that accompany the foreclosed identity. This being the case, an analysis of raw scores necessarily provides little information as to the constructs where this identity would wish to improve over the long term. Further, where a falling short is seen relative to me as I would like to be, the construct involved, problem solves, is neither core nor conflicted.

Regarding contra-identification, it is the case that we see only one entity at issue, a professional I don't admire. We turn to raw scores to reveal the behaviours of a professional I don't admire that the identity in question wishes to shun. Contra-identification, as described by Weinreich (2003) is 'the extent of one's contra-identification with another … the similarity between the qualities one attributes to the other and those from which one would wish to dissociate' (p. 58). Thus, in our approach to ISA

Table 3.3  Raw scores: idealistic identification

| Construct | Me as a Professional | Me as I would Like to be |
|---|---|---|
| accepts/judges | 4 | 4 |
| strong boundaries/struggles boundaries | 4 | 4 |
| shares knowledge/doesn't share | 1 | 1 |
| willing to learn/closed to learning | 2 | 2 |
| well informed/ poorly informed | 4 | 4 |
| creative/tried and tested | 4 | 4 |
| challenges/never challenges | 2 | 2 |
| instructs/reflection | 4 | 4 |
| processing emotions/hiding emotions | 3 | 4 |
| can be trusted/cannot be trusted | 4 | 4 |
| always right/makes mistakes | 1 | 1 |
| adapts to needs/rigid in approach | 4 | 4 |
| Problem solves/worries or avoids | 2 | 3 |

**Table 3.4** Raw scores: contra-identification

| Construct | Me as a Professional | Professional I Don't Admire |
|---|---|---|
| accepts/judges | 4 | -4 |
| strong boundaries/struggles boundaries | 4 | -4 |
| shares knowledge/doesn't share | 1 | -3 |
| willing to learn/closed to learning | 2 | 0 |
| well informed/ poorly informed | 4 | -1 |
| creative/tried and tested | 4 | -4 |
| challenges/never challenges | 2 | -3 |
| instructs/reflection | 4 | -4 |
| processing emotions/hiding emotions | 3 | -4 |
| can be trusted/cannot be trusted | 4 | 0 |
| always right/makes mistakes | 1 | 2 |
| adapts to needs/rigid in approach | 4 | -3 |
| Problem solves/worries or avoids | 2 | -4 |

analysis we are looking for those raw scores where the entity of contra-identification aligns to the negative poles of the constructs of an instrument. A comparison of the raw scores of me as a professional to a professional I don't admire ought to turn up behaviours the identity in question wishes to shun in the workplace (behaviours that might be explored in mentoring sessions) (Table 3.4).

For a professional I don't admire, behaviours along all but one of the constructs (always does it right/makes mistakes) are perceived negatively. The more extreme comparisons concern accepts/judges, strong boundaries/struggles to keep boundaries, creative/tried and tested, adapts to my needs/rigid in approach. These more extreme comparisons involve the 3 pressured constructs and a core construct (adapts to my needs). Questioning around the pressured constructs in particular may uncover reasons behind the contra-identification pattern.

## EMPATHETIC IDENTIFICATIONS

*Empathetic Identification: minimum value = 0.00, maximum value = 1.00 Whereas idealistic identifications represent long-term aspirations; empathetic identifications are of the here and now. Change in empathetic identifications across context and mood states reflects potential for change in behaviour.*

Current empathetic-identifications based in 'me as a professional' are: a public figure I admire (1.00), key adult female (1.00), a good friend (0.85)

Current empathetic identifications based in 'me outside of work' are: a public figure I admire (1.00), key adult female (1.00), a good friend (0.85)

Past Empathetic identification based in 'me as a trainee' are: a public figure I admire (1.00), key adult female (1.00), a good friend (0.91)

In the above, we see that the pattern of empathetic identification across the domains of the instrument involves the same entities. Over time, the empathetic identification pattern in the workplace has evolved to mirror that of a good friend to a lesser degree. The remaining empathetic identifications are remarkably consistent across the instrument's domains and over time. In regard to empathetic identification then, this hypothetical identity has shown similar behaviours over time. Further, in current times, there is little potential for behaviours to change when moving from the workplace to the home environment and vice versa.

## Conflicted Identification

*Conflicted identification: minimum value = 0.00, maximum value = 1.00*

*Conflicted identification in ISA references the combination of contra- and empathetic identification with significant others; being 'as' another while at the same time wishing to disassociate from those characteristics that are seen to be held in common.*

Current conflicted identification conflicts based in 'me as a professional' are: a public figure I don't admire (0.42), a person I no longer like (0.44)

Current conflicted identification based in 'me outside of work' are: a public figure I don't admire (0.42), a person I no longer like (0.44)

Past conflicted identification based in 'me as a trainee' are: a public figure I don't admire (0.46), a person I no longer like (0.44)

For this identity, the same entities (a public figure I don't admire and a person I no longer like) prove troublesome in work (both now and in the past) and outside of the workplace. Neither entity is the focus of idealistic or contra-identification. Further, these entities are not the subject of significant empathetic identification.

Conflicted identification with another references 'the degree of similarity between the qualities one attributes to the other, whether "good" or "bad" and those of one's current self-image' (Weinreich, 2003, p. 60). This being the case, we focus the examination of raw scores on the constructs where the entity of current self and the entity of conflicted identification lean toward the negatively rated poles of constructs (where the 2 entities align toward positively rated poles, the overlap ought not prove troublesome to the entity of current self). Table 3.5 presents raw scores for me as a professional and for the 2 entities of conflicted identification (a public figure I don't admire, and, a person I no longer like).

In the case of a foreclosed identity, entities of self are necessarily rated at a high and positive level. This being the case, we have to consider how we can adapt our approach to the examination of raw scores. We therefore turn to consider where me as a professional has the lowest ratings and the targets of conflicted identification have negative scores. The constructs where me as a professional scores lowest are, shares knowledge/doesn't share knowledge and always does it right/makes mistakes. A public figure I don't admire scores negatively for shares knowledge/ doesn't share knowledge (interestingly this entity has a maximally positive score for always does it right). A person I no longer like scores zero for always right/makes mistakes. Always does it right/makes mistakes is the most conflicted construct and it is a matter of note in Table 3.5. Assuming that this adaptation to the interpretation of raw scores proves correct, the suggestion is that always right/makes mistakes is likely a good place to begin a conversation to help this identity overcome the conflicted identifications.

## EVALUATION OF AND EGO INVOLVEMENT WITH OTHERS

*Evaluation minimum value = -1.00 maximum value = +1.00*
*Ego involvement minimum value = 0.00 maximum value = 5.00*
*Evaluation of others refers to a summation of the positive and negative scores associated with each entity. Entities as a result can have a positive or negative value for this parameter.*
*Ego involvement refers to the overall responsiveness to an entity in terms of the extensiveness in quantity (number of characteristics possessed) and strength (where the rating of each characteristic lies along the zero-centre scale) of the attributes they are rated as possessing.*

**Table 3.5** Raw scores: conflicted identification

| Construct | Me as a Professional | A Public Figure I Don't Admire | A Person I no longer Like |
|---|---|---|---|
| accepts/judges | 4 | 2 | 4 |
| strong boundaries/struggles boundaries | 4 | 0 | 4 |
| shares knowledge/doesn't share | 1 | -2 | 3 |
| willing to learn/closed to learning | 2 | -1 | 2 |
| well informed/ poorly informed | 4 | 1 | 1 |
| creative/tried and tested | 4 | 0 | 4 |
| challenges/never challenges | 2 | -4 | -1 |
| instructs/reflection | 4 | 2 | 4 |
| processing emotions/hiding emotions | 3 | -2 | -2 |
| can be trusted/cannot be trusted | 4 | -1 | -1 |
| always right/makes mistakes | 1 | 4 | 0 |
| adapts to needs/rigid in approach | 4 | 2 | 4 |
| Problem solves/worries or avoids | 2 | -4 | -1 |

## Entities of Primary Investigative Interest

A public figure I admire (evaluation of 0.87) (ego involvement: 3.91)
A public figure I don't admire (evaluation of -0.08) (ego: 4.35)
Key adult female (evaluation of 1.00) (ego: 5.00)
A good friend (evaluation of 0.87) (ego: 4.24)
A person I no longer like (evaluation of 0.37) (ego: 3.37)

Key adult female has maximal positive evaluation and maximal ego involvement. Ego involvement with all remaining entities of investigative interest is moderate. A public figure I admire has moderate positive evaluation as does a good friend. Even a person I no longer like has moderate positive evaluation. The remaining entity of investigative interest, a public figure I don't admire has moderately negative evaluation. These findings are in keeping with the remainder of this analysis. The identity of this investigation is most motivated to behave as the key adult female entity is perceived to behave. Fortunately, whilst at work this is an entity of empathetic identification which suggests that the identity feels able to behave as desired in the workplace.

## Evaluation of Self, Extent of Identity Diffusion, and Identity Variant

*Self-Evaluation: minimum value = -1.00, maximum value = 1.00*
*Identity Diffusion: minimum value = 0.00, maximum value = 1.00*
*Self-evaluation refers to measurements wherein characteristics associated with the various entities of self (me as a student teacher, me at work etc.) are compared to characteristics associated with the ideal aspirational self (me as I would like to be).*
*Identity diffusion in ISA is a measure of the extent of a person's conflicts of identification.*

**'Me as I would like to be'**
Self-evaluation:   0.89
Identity diffusion:   0.21
Identity variant: Defensive High Self-Regard
**'Me as I would least like to be'**
Self-evaluation:   -0.30
Identity diffusion:   0.38
Identity Variant: Indeterminate
**'Me, as trainee'**
Self-evaluation:   0.95
Identity diffusion: 0.23
Identity variant: Defensive High Self-Regard
**'Me, as a professional'**
Self–evaluation: 0.85
Identity Diffusion: 0.21
Identity Variant: Defensive High Self-Regard
**'Me, outside of work**
Self–evaluation: 0.72
Identity Diffusion: 0.21
Identity Variant: Indeterminate

Three of the entities of self are rated as defensive high self-regard. The remaining entities of self are indeterminate. Overall, we see a defensive high self-regard or foreclosed identity. To counsel the entities of self, an initial step would be to help this hypothetical identity recognise and register the conflicted identifications. Toward this end, try to facilitate understanding of why a public figure I don't admire and a person I no longer like might behave as perceived regarding the previously noted constructs: shares knowledge/ doesn't share knowledge and always right/makes mistakes.

Regarding performance in the workplace, me as a trainee and me as a professional are seen to perform at a higher level than me as I would like to be. Me as I would like to be is rated inappropriately high (above the intermediate component of Fig. 3.4). The suggestion is that there is (and was) an unrealistically high perception of performance in the workplace and that no or little room for improvement is seen in the future. Supervision to temper expectations for current and future workplace performance is recommended.

**Fig. 3.4** Representation of the ISA identity variants of the identity of Chap. 3

## Summary of ISA Report

The core constructs concern: struggles to keep boundaries, is creative, instructs, adapts to my needs, accepts, can be trusted. The first 3 of these listed constructs are pressured and they are also emotionally significant. The remaining listed constructs are of core structural pressure and other than, can be trusted, they are of high emotional significance. This hypothetical person is likely to be aware of the influence the core constructs (other than can be trusted) wield over their identity. Four of the constructs lie in the normative theme of the instrument (struggles to keep boundaries, creative, instructs, can be trusted). Two of the constructs lie in the restorative theme (accepts and adapts to my needs). If we consider the constructs within the normative theme which focusses on the more managerial aspects including ethics and quality issues, it appears from the ISA summary that this identity understands the importance of these constructs to the profession, suggesting a person with a rather fixed view of right and wrong as the primary focus of counselling supervision and the profession rather than a learning and development process (the formative function). The restorative function relates to the professional environment and it is clear that this identity values the professional environment in perhaps what could be viewed as a more practical sense rather than an environment for reflection and development.

The conflicted constructs concern: willing to learn, doesn't share knowledge, always does it right. They are associated with low (always does it right) to borderline-moderate emotional significance. The identity in question may not be aware that they represent issues. Two of the conflicted constructs lie in the formative theme of the instrument (always does it right is normative). The weighting of conflicted formative constructs might suggest that this identity struggles with this theme (however, note that always does it right is the most stressed of the conflicted constructs). The predominance of constructs in the formative theme (concerned with educational and learning aspects of supervision) indicates that this identity is not concerned with the personal development aspects of supervision (as indicated by the core constructs discussed). This could suggest the identity has fixed views on what a counsellor does/is and the purpose of counselling supervision. Viewing supervision as practical support to help the professional support clients within the professional guidelines rather than their own professional development.

A supervisor might begin counselling supervision by introducing questions that aim to uncover the nature of the issues around the most conflicted construct or constructs. A suitable opening question might be can you talk about the situations where you have struggled with the issue of making mistakes/always doing it right? To associate a conflicted construct with a core or pressured construct, try asking a question such as: how does being creative impact the notion of always being right versus making mistakes? Again, these indicate a concern for high self-regard and high self-competence, addressing skills and abilities important to the profession.

There is strong positive identification with a public figure I admire and key adult female. A good friend represents borderline high idealistic identification. In comparing me as a professional to me as I would like to be, note that me as a professional is rated positively in regard to a every construct of the instrument. Only in regard to problem solves/worries or avoids is me as a professional accorded a lower positive rating than me as I would like to be. It is the case then that the identity in question sees little room for improvement in the future. In terms of developing as a counselling professional, it is positive that the supervisee has a strong identification with the chosen profession and may even view counselling as a 'calling', as discussed in the introduction to the chapter. They clearly identify as a counsellor and view the profession as part of their self-concept, acting in terms of the group norms (Hogg & Terry, 2000).

Only a professional I don't admire is the subject of contra-identification. For this entity, all but one of the constructs (always does it right/makes mistakes) are perceived negatively. The comparison to me as a professional is most unfavourable regarding accepts/judges, strong boundaries/struggles to keep boundaries, creative/tried and tested, adapts to my needs/rigid in approach. These comparisons involve 3 pressured constructs and a core construct (adapts to my needs). Questioning around the pressured constructs may uncover reasons behind the contra-identification pattern and help the identity in question better empathise with the behaviours associated with a professional I don't admire.

Empathetic identifications across domain and time involve the same entities; a public figure I admire, key adult female and a good friend. Over time, the empathetic identification pattern in the workplace has evolved to mirror that of a good friend a little less. Empathetic identification with the remaining entities has been consistently high over time and across domains. There is little potential for behaviours to change when moving from the workplace to the home environment and vice versa.

Regarding conflicted identification, the same entities (a public figure I don't admire and a person I no longer like) prove troublesome in work (both now and in the past) and outside of the workplace. Neither entity is the focus of idealistic, contra or empathetic identification. Comparing raw scores for me as a professional and the entities of conflicted identification involves consideration of those constructs where me as a professional scored lowest (all constructs were rated positively for this entity). Shares knowledge/doesn't share knowledge and always does it right/makes mistake are the constructs of concern. A public figure I don't admire scores negatively for shares knowledge/doesn't share knowledge and has a maximally positive score for always does it right. A person I no longer like scores zero for always does it right/makes mistakes. Always does it right/ makes mistakes is the most conflicted construct and is likely then to be the place to begin a conversation to help the identity overcome conflicted identifications. This identity views themselves in the right profession, with a high level of perceived self-competence for the profession evident.

Key adult female has maximal positive evaluation and maximal ego involvement. Ego involvement with all remaining entities of investigative interest is moderate. A public figure I admire has moderate positive evaluation, as does a good friend. Even a person I no longer like has moderate positive evaluation. The remaining entity of investigative interest, a public figure I don't admire has moderately negative evaluations. These findings are in keeping with the other findings of this analysis. The identity of this investigation is most motivated to behave as the key adult female is perceived to behave. Fortunately, whilst at work, this is an entity of empathetic identification which suggests that the identity feels able to behave as desired in the workplace.

Three of the entities of self are rated as defensive high self-regard. The remaining entities of self are indeterminate. Overall this is a defensive high self-regard or foreclosed identity. Moving the entities of self toward the desired indeterminate variant of ISA helps the identity in question recognise the conflicted identifications noted above. That is, try to facilitate understanding of why a public figure I don't admire and a person I no longer like might behave as perceived regarding the previously noted constructs: shares knowledge/ doesn't share knowledge and always right/ makes mistakes.

In the workplace, me as a trainee and me as a professional are seen to perform at a higher level than me as I would like to be. Given that me as I would like to be is rated inappropriately high, it is likely that there is an unrealistically high perception of performance in the workplace, both now and in the past, and that no or little room for improvement is seen in the future. Supervision to temper expectations for current and future workplace performance is recommended.

## References

Bandura, A. (1977). Self-efficacy: Toward a unifying theory of behavioral change. *Psychological Review*, *84*(2), 191–215. https://doi.org/10.1037/0033-295X.84.2.191

Barnett, M. D., Moore, J. M., & Garza, C. J. (2019). Meaning in life and self-esteem help hospice nurses withstand prolonged exposure to death. *Journal of Nursing Management*, *27*(4), 775–780. https://doi.org/10.1111/jonm.12737

Cleary, D. (2019). Spirituality in the recovery process of addiction – Is there an impact on the counsellor? *Irish Association for Counselling and Psychotherapy*, *19*(1), 14–19.

Coulson, J., Stoyles, G., & Oades, L. (2013). Calling in childrearing: Promoting meaningful, purposeful living in family life. In J. Sinnott (Ed.), *Positive psychology* (pp. 3–18). Springer.

Demirbaş-Çelik, N., & Keklik, İ. (2019). Personality factors and meaning in life: The mediating role of competence, relatedness and autonomy. *Journal of Happiness Studies*, *20*(4), 995–1013. https://doi.org/10.1007/s10902-018-9984-0

Edwards, M. E., & Van Tongeren, D. R. (2020). Meaning mediates the association between suffering and well-being. *The Journal of Positive Psychology*, *15*(6), 722–733. https://doi.org/10.1080/17439760.2019.1651890

Hardiman, P., & Simmonds, J. G. (2013). Spiritual well-being, burnout and trauma in counsellors and psychotherapists. *Mental Health, Religion & Culture*, *16*(10), 1044–1055. https://doi.org/10.1080/13674676.2012.732560

Harris, K. J., Kacmar, K., & Zivnuska, S. (2007). An investigation of abusive supervision as a predictor of performance and the meaning of work as a moderator of the relationship. *The Leadership Quarterly*, *18*, 252–263. https://doi.org/10.1016/j.leaqua.2007.03.007

Hogg, M. A., & Terry, D. J. (2000). Social identity and self-categorization processes in organizational context. *Academy of Management Review*, *25*, 121–140.

Hurst, R., & Prescott, J. (2021). Counselling as a calling: Meaning in life and perceived self- competence in counselling students. *Counselling and Psychotherapy Research Journal*. https://doi.org/10.1002/capr.12406

Joseph, S. (2016). *Authentic: How to be yourself and why it matters*. Piatkus Little-Brown.

Kasser, T., & Ryan, R. M. (1993). A dark side of the American dream: Correlates of financial success as a central life aspiration. *Journal of Personality and Social Psychology, 65*, 410–422.

Leising, D., Borkenau, P., Zimmermann, J., Roski, C., Leonhardt, A., & Schutz, A. (2013). Positive self-regard and claim to leadership: Two fundamental forms of self-evaluation. *European Journal of Personality, 27*, 565–579. https://doi.org/10.1002/per.1924

Lippe, M., Davis, A., Threadgill, H., & Ricamato, A. (2020). Development of a new measure to assess primary palliative care perceived competence. *Nurse Educator, 45*(2), 106–110.

Marcia, J. E. (1966). Development and validation of ego-identity status. *Journal of Personality and Social Psychology, 3*, 551–558.

Rogers, C. R. (1961). *On becoming a person.* Constable.

Russo-Netzer, P., Sinai, M., & Zeevi, M. (2020). Meaning in life and work among counsellors: A qualitative exploration. *British Journal of Guidance & Counselling, 48*(2), 209–226. https://doi.org/10.1080/03069885.2019.1625026

Ryan, R. M., & Deci, E. L. (2000). Self-determination theory and the facilitation of intrinsic motivation, social development, and well-being. *American Psychologist, 55*, 68–78.

Seligman, M. E. (2004). *Authentic happiness: Using the new positive psychology to realize your potential for lasting fulfillment.* Simon and Schuster.

Weinreich, P. (2003). Theory and practice: Introduction. In Weinreich & Saunderson (Eds.), *Analysing identity: Clinical, societal and cross-cultural contexts* (pp. 1–5). Taylor and Francis, Routledge, and Psychology Press.

CHAPTER 4

# The Diffuse High Self-Regard Identity Variant

**Abstract** Continuing in the vein of Chaps. 2 and 3, we here present an illustrative ISA analysis for the diffuse high self-regard identity variant. Here again, theoretical data was created to generate the desired identity variant type and once again, we provide raw scores in figures and tables so that the reader can better discern our approach to ISA analysis.

**Keywords** Diffuse high self-regard identity variant • Identity diffusion • Marcia's identity development theory • Career motivation • Career resilience • Career insight • Career identity • Career development patterns • Self-concept

## INTRODUCTION

Identity diffusion is viewed as a lack of integration of the concept of self and significant others. This results in a loss of capacity for self-definition and commitment to values, goals or relationships, and a painful sense of incoherence. According to Marcia (1966), individuals with a lack of commitment and exploration of identity are diffused. Identity diffusion has been viewed as a starting point of identity formation (Waterman, 1982). Identity diffusion differs between individuals (Kroger & Marcia, 2011);

© The Author(s), under exclusive license to Springer Nature Switzerland AG 2022
G. Passmore, J. Prescott, *Using an ISA Mobile App for Professional Development*, https://doi.org/10.1007/978-3-030-99071-8_4

however, individuals in identity diffusion have previously been described as being less autonomous and more likely to be sensitive to external pressures when compared to the other stages of Marcia's identity development theory (identity achievement, moratorium and foreclosure) (Marcia et al., 1993).

Linking this identity to the career identity literature, it is worth briefly discussing the importance of career motivation to commitment and identification. According to London and Stumpf (1982), there are three basic dimensions of career motivations: career resilience, career insight and career identity. The career resilience dimension provides drive to overcome obstacles faced in a given career. Career insight allows an individual to understand themselves in terms of their career and work environment and career identity allows for the individual to channel their behaviour toward the objectives of their chosen career. Quigley and Tymon (2006) suggest that from these three dimensions, four career development patterns emerge: healthy, redirected, intervening self-doubt and lastly, breaking away from an ineffective pattern. It is clear that motivation and identifying with a career are closely linked. Indeed, research suggests that individuals are motivated to maintain their self-identity in the workplace (Haslam et al., 2000). Other research has considered the importance of personality traits with career motivation, suggesting increased job satisfaction in individuals able to express their personality traits within their job and careers (Schmitt et al., 2003). Linking back to the research on counselling careers being a calling for some individuals and the potential meaning individuals give to work/careers, we can see close links between identification and motivation. In order to identify with a profession, an individual's self-concept needs to overlap with the values and goals of the profession. A profession can represent a social category, with the job role viewed as an important social category to many (Hogg & Terry, 2000). Identification involves an individual incorporating the norms and values of a profession and integrates their own beliefs about a profession into their own identity. Given this, withdrawal from a profession or indeed an organisation would be therefore detrimental to an individual's self-concept, and therefore they are less likely to leave. Research has therefore found identification to be associated with low staff turnover and increased job satisfaction (Van Dick et al., 2004). Much of the research on professional identification has focussed on social identity theory and self-categorisation theory due to the emphasis on people's positionality in terms of social groups (see Tajfel, 1978; Tajfel & Turner, 1979; Turner et al., 1987 for more insight into these theories).

## Structural Pressure and Emotional Significance

*Emotional Significance: Minimum value = 0.00, maximum value = 100.00.*
*The emotional significance of a construct used in appraisal of the counsellor's social world is defined as the strength of affect associated with the expression of the construct. The index of standardised emotional significance can range from 0.00 (no significance) to 10.00 (maximal significance).*
*Structural Pressure: Minimum value = -100, maximum value = +100*
*Structural Pressure reflects the consistency with which a construct is used to evaluate entities. High Structural Pressure constructs are used in a consistent manner to evaluate others. They represent the core, stable evaluative dimensions of the identity under consideration. Low Structural Pressure constructs are used to evaluate others in different ways depending on circumstance and context. Low Structural Pressure suggests an area of stress and indecision; a conflicted dimension liable to poor decision making* (Table 4.1).

Core constructs concern: leads to hiding emotions, shares knowledge, always does it right, worries or avoids. The first and last of these listed constructs lie in the restore theme of the instrument. Shares knowledge is a formative construct and always does it right is normative. All of these constructs are core (none are pressured). Facilitates processing emotions has maximum emotional significance for the hypothetical identity in question. One construct (always does it right) is associated with high-level emotional significance and one (shares knowledge) is borderline high. Worries or avoids is associated with moderate emotional significance. There is a strong potential that the identity is aware that leads to hiding

**Table 4.1** Core and conflicted values and beliefs

| Pole 1 | Pole 2 | SP | ES |
|---|---|---|---|
| Core constructs | | | |
| facilitates processing emotions | leads to hiding emotions | 79.42 | 10.00 |
| shares knowledge | doesn't share knowledge | 70.58 | 8.31 |
| always does it right | makes mistakes | 69.19 | 8.87 |
| problem solves | worries or avoids | 62.52 | 6.25 |
| Conflicted constructs | | | |
| adapts to my needs | is quite rigid in approach | 23.23 | 7.58 |
| is creative | sticks to the tried and tested | 13.91 | 6.08 |

emotions influences behaviour and reasonable potential that there is awareness of the influence of the constructs that are associated with high-level and borderline high emotional significance. The construct of moderate (worries or avoids) emotional significance may or may not be on the identity's radar.

The conflicted constructs are: is quite rigid in approach and is creative. The first of these constructs is a restore construct and creative is normative. No one theme dominates the conflicted constructs and can be considered a target for counselling. Not one of the conflicted constructs is sufficiently stressed as to merit a contradictory ISA rating. Is quite rigid in approach is associated with moderate-level emotional significance. Is creative is associated with low-level (borderline moderate) emotional significance. Consequently, this identity may not be aware that the conflicted constructs represent issues. The most stressed construct is likely the construct that counselling supervision might best tackle first, so begin by introducing questions that aim to uncover the nature of the issues around it. For example, 'can you talk about situations you have encountered where you have struggled over whether it was better to solve a problem or worry/avoid tackling it'? Issues associated with this construct that arise during supervision sessions can be tackled by drawing up plans and then monitoring behaviour. The same approach to questioning could be applied to 'is quite rigid in approach'.

To associate a conflicted construct with a core or pressured construct, consider the construct leads to hiding emotions and the constructive is quite rigid in approach. A suitable question might be, how might behaviours that lead to hiding emotions impact a person's ability to adapt to your needs. Proceed thereafter with a discussion around this question.

## IDEALISTIC AND CONTRA-IDENTIFICATIONS

*Idealistic Identification: minimum value = 0.00, maximum value = 1.00*
*Contra-Identification: minimum value = 0.00, maximum value = 1.00*
*Idealistic identifications (II) point to a person's role models. They indicate the characteristics a person will seek to emulate over the long term.*
*Contra-identifications (CI) indicate negative role models. Those who possess characteristics from which a person wishes to dissociate* (Table 4.2).

The identity of this chapter exhibits strong positive identification with a professional I admire and a good friend. Turning to raw scores,

## 4 THE DIFFUSE HIGH SELF-REGARD IDENTITY VARIANT

**Table 4.2** Idealistic and contra-identifications

| Entity | II | CI |
|---|---|---|
| A professional I admire | 0.62 | |
| A good friend | 0.62 | |
| A professional I don't admire | | 0.92 |

**Table 4.3** Raw scores: idealistic identification

| Construct | Me as a Professional | A professional I admire |
|---|---|---|
| accepts/judges | 3 | 1 |
| strong boundaries/struggles boundaries | -2 | 1 |
| shares knowledge/doesn't share | 4 | -1 |
| willing to learn/closed to learning | 3 | -3 |
| well informed/ poorly informed | 3 | 0 |
| creative/tried and tested | 0 | 3 |
| challenges/never challenges | 0 | 4 |
| instructs/reflection | 2 | -3 |
| processing emotions/hiding emotions | 3 | 4 |
| can be trusted/cannot be trusted | 2 | -2 |
| always right/makes mistakes | 4 | 4 |
| adapts to needs/rigid in approach | 2 | 1 |
| Problem solves/worries or avoids | 2 | 1 |

differences in the 'behaviours seen in me as a professional' and 'a professional I admire' ought to point to behaviours that the identity wishes to aspire toward over the long term (Table 4.3).

The raw scores suggest that the identity would like to see me as a professional behaving more creatively, be more challenging, and be better able to hide emotions. Consideration of constructs where me as I would like to be scores negatively suggests that me as a professional would wish to be better able to maintain boundaries, be more willing to learn, invoke more instruction and less reflection and be trusted more. Referring back to Table 4.1, we see that hiding or processing emotions is the primary core construct and that it is of maximum emotional significance. Further, we see that being creative or sticking to the tried and tested is the most conflicted construct. The finding regarding creative/tried and tested indicates that it will make for an effective area of focus for supervision purposes.

Turning to the contra-identification pattern, we see only one entity at issue, a professional I don't admire. Comparison of the raw scores of me as a professional to a professional I don't admire ought to turn up behaviours that the identity of investigation wishes to shun in the workplace (Table 4.4).

For a professional I don't admire, all but one of the constructs is rated negatively and all of the constructs are rated negative relative to me as a professional. Rather than reporting all of the negatively rated behaviours we will focus on matters where the differences between me as a professional and a professional I don't admire are the greatest: doesn't share knowledge, willing to learn, is well informed, leads to hiding emotions, and makes mistakes. It is recommended that where counselling focuses on this contra-identification pattern, questions be posed that surround the 3 core constructs at issue: leads to hiding emotions, shares knowledge, and makes mistakes. It may also be worth questioning why 'me as a professional' prefers the pole 'closed to learning' as this is not an expected finding.

Table 4.4 Raw scores: contra-identification

| Construct | Me as a Professional | Professional I Don't Admire |
|---|---|---|
| accepts/judges | 3 | 2 |
| strong boundaries/struggles boundaries | -2 | -3 |
| shares knowledge/doesn't share | 4 | -3 |
| willing to learn/closed to learning | 3 | -4 |
| well informed/ poorly informed | 3 | -4 |
| creative/tried and tested | 0 | -2 |
| challenges/never challenges | 0 | -4 |
| instructs/reflection | 2 | -3 |
| processing emotions/hiding emotions | 3 | -4 |
| can be trusted/cannot be trusted | 2 | -3 |
| always right/makes mistakes | 4 | -3 |
| adapts to needs/rigid in approach | 2 | -4 |
| Problem solves/worries or avoids | 2 | -2 |

## Empathetic Identifications

*Empathetic Identification: minimum value = 0.00, maximum value = 1.00*
Whereas idealistic identifications represent long-term aspirations; empathetic identifications are of the here and now. Change in empathetic identifications across context and mood states reflects potential for change in behaviour.
Current empathetic identifications based in 'me as a professional' are: a public figure I admire (0.55)
Current empathetic identifications based in 'me outside of work' are: a public figure I admire (0.55)
Past Empathetic identification based on 'me as a trainee' are: none

In the above, we see that significant empathetic identification in the workplace has changed over time. In the workplace and at home though, the same degree of empathetic identification is present for the same entity, a public figure I admire. In current times, this identity shows little potential for behaviour change in moving between the work and home domains.

## Conflicted Identification

*Conflicted identification: minimum value = 0.00, maximum value = 1.00*
Conflicted identification in ISA references the combination of contra- and empathetic identification with significant others; being 'as' another while at the same time wishing to disassociate from those characteristics that are seen to be held in common.
Current conflicted identification-conflicts based in 'me as a professional' are: a person I no longer like (0.47), a public figure I don't admire (0.47), a public figure I admire (0.46)
Current conflicted identifications based in 'me outside of work' are: a person I no longer like (0.47), a public figure I don't admire (0.47), a public figure I admire (0.46)
Past conflicted identifications based on 'me as a trainee' are: a professional I don't admire (0.53)

Here we need to state that the Ipseus report for this identity indicates that significant conflicted identification begins at (0.56). It is the case then that there are no significant identification conflicts at issue. That said, a number of entities are associated with moderate identification conflict.

**Table 4.5** Raw scores: conflicted identification

| Construct | Me as a Professional | A Public Figure I Admire | A Public Figure I Don't Admire | A Person I no longer Like |
|---|---|---|---|---|
| accepts/judges | 3 | 3 | -1 | 3 |
| strong boundaries/struggles boundaries | -2 | -2 | -2 | -2 |
| shares knowledge/doesn't share | 4 | 3 | -1 | -3 |
| willing to learn/closed to learning | 3 | -3 | -3 | -4 |
| well informed/ poorly informed | 3 | -4 | 2 | -4 |
| creative/tried and tested | 0 | 4 | 0 | 4 |
| challenges/never challenges | 0 | 1 | 4 | 3 |
| instructs/reflection | 2 | -2 | -4 | -2 |
| processing emotions/hiding emotions | 3 | 4 | -4 | 4 |
| can be trusted/cannot be trusted | 2 | -2 | -3 | 2 |
| always right/makes mistakes | 4 | 3 | 4 | -1 |
| adapts to needs/rigid in approach | 2 | 0 | 4 | -4 |
| Problem solves/worries or avoids | 2 | 2 | -3 | -1 |

Raw scores associated with the entities of moderate identification conflict are considered below (Table 4.5).

When we examine where 'me as a professional' and the entities of identification conflict present with negative raw scores only one construct is at issue: has strong boundaries/struggles to keep boundaries. We suggest that should a counsellor consider that there is a need to help this identity overcome the moderate identification conflicts, questions should be posed that explore issues around this construct.

## EVALUATION OF AND EGO INVOLVEMENT WITH OTHERS

*Evaluation minimum value = -1.00 maximum value = +1.00*
*Ego involvement minimum value = 0.00 maximum value = 5.00*

*Evaluation of others refers to a summation of the positive and negative scores associated with each entity. Entities as a result can have a positive or negative value for this parameter.*
*Ego involvement refers to the overall responsiveness to an entity in terms of the extensiveness in quantity (number of characteristics possessed) and strength (where the rating of each characteristic lies along the zero-center scale) of the attributes they are rated as possessing.*

## Entities of Primary Investigative Interest

A professional I don't admire (evaluation of -1.00) (ego-involvement: 5.00)
A professional I admire (evaluation of 0.29) (ego-involvement: 3.41)
A public figure I don't admire (evaluation of -0.20) (ego: 4.27)
A public figure I admire (evaluation of 0.20) (ego: 4.02)
A person I no longer like (evaluation of -0.41) (ego: 4.51)

This identity exhibits moderate evaluation of all entities of investigative interest other than a professional I don't admire (maximally negative). The latter entity is also the subject of maximal ego involvement and the lone entity of contra-identification. Ego involvement with the remaining entities is moderate. It is the case then that the identity is most motivated to avoid behaving as per the perceived behaviours of a professional I don't admire.

## Evaluation of Self, Extent of Identity Diffusion, and Identity Variant

*Self-Evaluation: minimum value = -1.00, maximum value = 1.00*
*Identity Diffusion: minimum value = 0.00, maximum value = 1.00*
*Self-evaluation refers to measurements wherein characteristics associated with the various entities of self (me as a student teacher, me at work etcetera) are compared to characteristics associated with the ideal aspirational self (me as I would like to be).*
*Identity diffusion in ISA is a measure of the extent of a person's conflicts of identification* (Fig. 4.1)

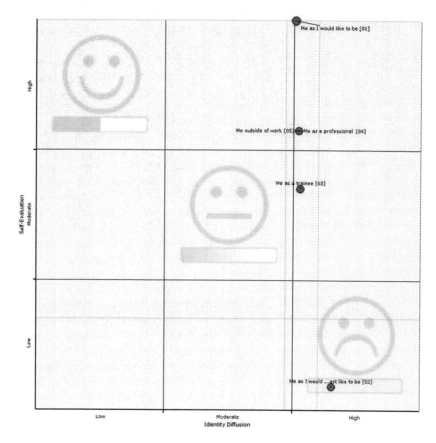

**Fig. 4.1** Representation of the ISA identity variants of the identity of Chap. 4

*'Me as I would like to be'*
Self-evaluation: 1.00
Identity diffusion: 0.42
Identity variant: Diffuse High Self-Regard
*'Me as I would least like to be'*
Self-evaluation: −0.78
Identity diffusion: 0.59
Identity Variant: Crisis

*'Me, as trainee'*
Self-evaluation: 0.62
Identity diffusion: 0.44
Identity variant: Diffusion
*'Me, as a professional'*
Self-evaluation: 0.83
Identity diffusion: 0.43
Identity Variant: Diffuse High Self-Regard
*'Me, outside of work*
Self-evaluation: 0.83
Identity Diffusion: 0.43
Identity Variant: Diffuse High Self-Regard

The striking finding for this identity is that three of the five entities of self are rated as diffuse high-self-regard. That is, the identity recognises a high level of conflicted identifications and has a tendency for high self-evaluation. For me as a professional, the self-evaluation rating is beneath that of me as I would like to be as is the self-evaluation rating of me outside work. This suggests that the identity sees room for improved performance at work (and outside work). However, the self-evaluation of me as a professional (and me outside work) is higher than desired, which indicates that difficulties may be encountered attaining future improvement. Adding to the conclusion that future improvements in behaviour may not be readily attained is the finding that me as I would like to be has a maximum positive self-evaluation. Supervision to temper expectations for current and future workplace performance is recommended. Supervision to lower the moderate conflicted identifications is also recommended to help shift the entities of self toward the indeterminate rating.

## Summary of ISA Report

Core constructs concern: leads to hiding emotions, shares knowledge, always does it right, worries or avoids. The first and last of these constructs lie in the restorative theme of the instrument. Shares knowledge is a formative construct and always does it right is normative. All of these constructs are core. Facilitates processing emotions has maximum emotional significance. One construct (always does it right) is associated with high-level emotional significance and one (shares knowledge) is borderline high. Worries or avoids is associated with moderate emotional significance.

There is good potential that the identity is aware that leads to hiding emotions influences behaviour and reasonable potential that there is awareness of the influence of the constructs that are associated with high-level and borderline high emotional significance. The construct of moderate (worries or avoids) emotional significance may or may not be on the identity's radar.

The conflicted constructs are: is quite rigid in approach (restorative theme) and is creative (normative theme). No one theme dominates the conflicted constructs. This is quite different to the identity discussed in Chap. 2 and suggests a more rounded identity in terms of the profession and the purpose, and perhaps highlights the benefits of counselling supervision. Is quite rigid in approach is associated with moderate-level emotional significance. Is creative is associated with low-level (borderline moderate) emotional significance. This identity may not be aware that the conflicted constructs represent issues. This highlights the potential the ISA approach has from a professional development point of view, uncovering avenues for exploration to further understand and explore issues of potential concern within a professional identity. The most stressed construct is likely the construct that counselling supervision can best tackle, so begin by introducing questions that aim to uncover the nature of the issues around it. A suitable opening question might be 'can you talk about situations you have encountered where you have struggled over whether it was better to solve a problem or worry/avoid tackling it'? A suitable question for associating a conflicted construct with a core construct consideration might be, how might behaviours that lead to hiding emotions impact a person's ability to adapt to your needs.

There is a strong positive identification with a professional I admire and a good friend. Long-term aspirations include behaving more creatively, exhibiting more challenging behaviours, and better hiding of emotions, being better able to maintain boundaries, being more willing to learn, invoking more instruction and less reflection being trusted more. Hiding or processing emotions is the primary core construct of the identity and it is of maximum emotional significance. This is of particular relevance to a counselling professional and highlights the recognition of perceived self-competence of the identity and again, as with the identity in Chap. 3, could suggest the identity views the profession of counselling as a calling rather than a job. Linking to identity theory, it is clear this identity views being a counsellor as core to their identity and part of their self-concept (Hogg & Terry, 2000). Being creative or sticking to the tried and tested is the most conflicted construct. This may suggest the identity views certain skills and attitudes as core to the profession. Focus supervision on these constructs to help the identity attain aspirant behaviours.

Only one entity is subject to contra-identification, a professional I don't admire. For this entity all but one of the constructs is rated negatively and all of them are rated negative relative to me as a professional. The negative ratings are greatest regarding: doesn't share knowledge, willing to learn, is well informed, leads to hiding emotions, and makes mistakes. Focus counselling supervision on the 3 core constructs at issue: leads to hiding emotions, shares knowledge, and makes mistakes. It may also be worth questioning why me as a professional prefers the unconventional pole closed to learning. This may again suggest that this identity believes they have the skills and attitudes as well as identifies with the profession and therefore does not view the need to develop further. It could also perhaps suggest that this identity is less open to learning and developing through the supervision process as the identity discussed in Chap. 2. When considering the literature surrounding identity development and stages of identity, this finding may also show a lack of integration of the self with significant others, as posited by Marcia (1966) for an identity in diffusion.

Empathetic identification in the workplace has changed over time. In the workplace and at home though, the same degree of empathetic identification is present for a public figure I admire. In current times, this identity shows little potential for behaviour change when moving between the work and home domains.

There are no significant identification conflicts for this identity. Therefore, this identity is strongly identified with the profession and will no doubt be committed to the profession (Ashforth & Mael, 1989; Elsbach, 1999) with strong job satisfaction (Van Dick et al., 2004). A number of entities are associated with moderate identification conflict. The latter has resulted in entities of self in the Diffuse High Self-Regard Variant of ISA. The lone construct at issue regarding conflicted identification is: has strong boundaries/struggles to keep boundaries. Pose questions that explore issues around this construct. Perhaps a focus on what it is about boundaries as a counselling professional raises issues for them.

The entities of investigative interest are: public figure I admire, public figure I don't admire, professional I admire, professional I don't admire, and a person I no longer like. There is moderate evaluation of all entities of investigative interest other than a professional I don't admire (maximally negative). The latter entity is also the subject of maximal ego involvement and the lone entity of contra-identification. Ego involvement with the remaining entities is moderate. The identity is most motivated to avoid behaving as per the perceived behaviours of a professional I don't admire. Again, this leads to a suggestion of strong commitment to the profession. However, from a supervision and professional development point of view, it would be interesting to consider the future development of the identity and how they adapt to changes in the workplace and profession.

Three of the five entities of self are rated as diffuse high-self-regard. That is, there is a high level of conflicted identifications and a a tendency for high self-evaluation. While room for improvement is seen for me as a professional and me outside work, these entities, like me as I would like to be, have self-evaluation values that are too high. This perhaps suggests a lack of commitment and exploration of the individual as a counselling professional and the identity of this role. Supervision to temper expectations for current and future workplace performance is recommended. Supervision to lower the moderate conflicted identifications is also recommended to help shift the entities of self toward the indeterminate rating.

## References

Ashforth, B. E., & Mael, F. A. (1989). Social Identity theory and the organization. *Academy of Management Review, 14*(1), 20–39.

Haslam, S. A., Powel, L. C., & Turner, J. C. (2000). Social identity, self-categorization, and work motivation: Rethinking the contribution of the group to positive and sustainable organizational outcomes. *International Review of Applied Psychology, 49,* 319–339.

Hogg, M. A., & Terry, D. J. (2000). Social identity and self-categorization processes in organizational context. *Academy of Management Review, 25,* 121–140.

Kroger, J., & Marcia, J. E. (2011). The identity statuses: Origins, meanings, and interpretations. In S. J. Schwartz, K. Luyckx, & V. L. Vignoles (Eds.), *Handbook of identity theory and research* (pp. 31–53). Springer. https://doi.org/10.1007/978-1-4419-7988-9_2

London, M., & Stumpf, S. A. (1982). *Managing careers.* Addison-Wesley.

Marcia, J. E. (1966). Development and validation o ego-identity status. *Journal of Personality and Social Psychology, 3*(1966), 551–558. https://doi.org/10.1037/h0023281

Marcia, J. E., Waterman, A. S., Mattesson, D. R., Archer, S. L., & Orlofsky, J. L. (Eds.). (1993). *Ego identity. A handbook for psychosocial research.* Springer-Verlag.

Quigley, N. R., & Tymon, W. G. (2006). Toward an integrated model of intrinsic motivation and career self-management. *Career Development International, 11*(6), 522–543.

Schmitt, N., Cortina, J. M., Ingerick, M. J., & Wiechmann, D. (2003). Personnel selection and employee performance. In W. C. Borman, D. Ilgen, & R. J. Klimoski (Eds.), *Handbook of psychology* (Vol. 12, pp. 77–106). Wiley.

Tajfel, H. (Ed.). (1978). *Differentiation between social groups: Studies in the social psychology of inter-group relations.* Academic Press.

Tajfel, H., & Turner, J. C. (1979). An integrative theory of social conflict. In W. Austen & S. Worchel (Eds.), *The social psychology of inter-group relations* (2nd ed.). Nelson Hall.

Turner, J. C., Hogg, M. A., Oakes, P. J., Reicher, P. J., & Wetherall, M. S. (1987). *Rediscovering the social group: A self-categorization.* Blackwell.

Van Dick, R., Wagner, U., Stellmacher, J., & Christ, O. (2004). The utility of a broader conceptualization of organizational identification: Which aspects really matter? *Journal of Occupational and Organizational Psychology, 77,* 171–191.

Waterman, A. S. (1982). Identity development from adolescence to adulthood: An extension of theory and a review of research. *Developmental Psychology, 18,* 341–358. https://doi.org/10.1037/0012-1649.18.3.341

CHAPTER 5

# The Crisis Variant

**Abstract** Here we present an illustrative ISA analysis for the identity in crisis in the same manner as earlier chapters.

**Keywords** Crisis identity variant • Identity development theory • Identity confusion • Identity deficit • Identity conflict • Professional development • Technology support • Stress and burnout

## INTRODUCTION

Erikson's (1956) identity development theory views identity across the lifespan on a continuum from a firm identity to a confused identity. Erikson was among the first theorists to put forth a theory of identity development. Erikson's concept of identity is multidimensional and extensive in its scope and coverage. Erikson spoke of cognitive, moral, social, and cultural aspects of identity, among many others (Schwartz, 2001). In 1968, Erikson also posited that identity confusion can also be on a continuum from one end of mild confusion such as deciding on a course to take at the university, to the other end of aggravated confusion, which could be a feeling as though one's life lacks purpose (Schwartz, 2001). In terms of identities in crisis, early identity theorists identified two types of identity crisis, an identity deficit (motivation crisis) and identity conflict

© The Author(s), under exclusive license to Springer Nature Switzerland AG 2022
G. Passmore, J. Prescott, *Using an ISA Mobile App for Professional Development*, https://doi.org/10.1007/978-3-030-99071-8_5

(legitimation crisis) (Baumeister et al., 1985). Within the former, an identity deficit, the individual, the person, struggles to establish personal goals and values. In the latter, an identity conflict, the person has several commitments with conflicting behaviours. Kernberg (1978) viewed an individual's identity crisis as being a result of the discrepancy between shifting physical and psychological experiences, as well as a widening gap between self-perception and the experiences of others' perceptions of the self. This chapter will take a look at hypothetical data showing an identity in crisis.

## STRUCTURAL PRESSURE AND EMOTIONAL SIGNIFICANCE

*Emotional Significance: Minimum value = 0.00, maximum value = 100.00*
*The emotional significance of a construct used in appraisal of the counsellor's social world is defined as the strength of affect associated with the expression of the construct. The index of standardised emotional significance can range from 0.00 (no significance) to 10.00 (maximal significance).*
*Structural Pressure: Minimum value = -100, maximum value = +100*
*Structural Pressure reflects the consistency with which a construct is used to evaluate entities. High Structural Pressure constructs are used in a consistent manner to evaluate others. They represent the core, stable evaluative dimensions of the identity under consideration. Low Structural Pressure constructs are used to evaluate others in different ways depending on circumstance and context. Low Structural Pressure suggests an area of stress and indecision; a conflicted dimension liable to poor decision making* (Table 5.1).

Core constructs concern: struggles to keep boundaries, is willing to learn, worries or avoids, can be trusted, is well informed, accepts, leads to hiding emotions. These constructs are distributed fairly evenly across the 3 themes of the instrument. Is willing to learn, and is well informed are formative constructs; struggles to keep boundaries and can be trusted are normative; and accepts, leads to processing emotions and problem solves are restorative. None of the constructs are pressured, all of them are core. Struggles to maintain boundaries is associated with maximal emotional significance. The emotional significance of the remaining core constructs is moderate. There is good potential that the identity at hand is aware that struggles to maintain boundaries influences behaviour. It may or may not be the case that the identity is aware of those constructs that are associated with moderate emotional significance.

**Table 5.1** Core and conflicted values and beliefs

| Pole 1 | Pole 2 | SP | ES |
|---|---|---|---|
| Core constructs | | | |
| has strong boundaries | *struggles to keep boundaries* | 85.32 | 10.00 |
| *is willing to learn* | Is closed to learning | 77.01 | 8.07 |
| problem solves | *worries or avoids* | 76.85 | 7.68 |
| can be trusted | cannot be trusted | 75.82 | 7.77 |
| *is well informed* | is poorly informed | 73.12 | 7.31 |
| *Accepts* | Judges | 71.99 | 7.2 |
| facilitates processing emotions | *leads to hiding emotions* | 66.11 | 8.47 |
| Conflicted constructs | | | |
| always does it right | *makes mistakes* | 39.34 | 8.47 |
| *shares knowledge* | doesn't share knowledge | 39.07 | 5.53 |
| *adapts to my needs* | is quite rigid in approach | 30.28 | 6.43 |
| Challenges | never challenges | 3.83 | 6.19 |

The conflicted constructs are: makes mistakes, shares knowledge, adapts to my needs and challenges. Like the core constructs, the conflicted constructs are distributed fairly evenly across the themes of the instrument. Shares knowledge is formative, challenges and makes mistakes are normative, and, adapts to my needs is restorative. Not one of the conflicted constructs is sufficiently stressed as to merit a contradictory ISA rating. All of the conflicted constructs are associated with moderate emotional significance and as such the hypothetical identity may not be aware that they represent issues. The tack we recommend for counselling then is to begin with questioning around the most stressed construct. A suitable opening question might be 'can you speak to situations where you have struggled over whether to mount a challenge or not?' Thereafter, we recommend proceeding as per prior chapters, drawing up plans to improve behaviour around the construct and monitoring subsequent behaviour. The same approach to questioning could be applied to the remaining conflicted constructs.

To associate a conflicted construct with a core or pressured construct, consider the construct challenges/never challenges and the construct has strong boundaries/struggles to keep boundaries. A suitable question might be 'is it the case that never challenging a situation or situations can interfere with your ability to maintain boundaries'. Continue after posing the question with discussion around it.

## Idealistic and Contra-identifications

*Idealistic Identification: minimum value = 0.00, maximum value = 1.00*
*Contra-Identification: minimum value = 0.00, maximum value = 1.00*
Idealistic identifications (II) point to a person's role models. They indicate the characteristics a person will seek to emulate over the long term.
Contra-identifications (CI) indicate negative role models. Those who possess characteristics from which a person wishes to dissociate (Table 5.2).

The identity of this chapter exhibits strong positive identification with the key adult female and a good friend. Given that we are interested in long-term behavioural aspirations in the workplace during counselling sessions, we will focus on a comparison of the raw scores of me as a professional and a professional I admire to reveal behaviours that the identity wishes to aspire toward over the long term. A professional I admire is associated with moderate idealistic identification (0.54) (Table 5.3).

**Table 5.2** Idealistic and contra-identifications

| Entity | II | CI |
|---|---|---|
| Key adult female | 0.92 | |
| A good friend | 0.85 | |
| A professional I don't admire | | 1.00 |

**Table 5.3** Raw scores: idealistic identification

| Construct | Me as a Professional | A professional I admire |
|---|---|---|
| accepts/judges | -4 | 1 |
| strong boundaries/struggles boundaries | -4 | 1 |
| shares knowledge/doesn't share | -4 | -1 |
| willing to learn/closed to learning | -2 | 2 |
| well informed/ poorly informed | -2 | 0 |
| creative/tried and tested | -3 | 3 |
| challenges/never challenges | -2 | -1 |
| instructs/reflection | -4 | 0 |
| processing emotions/hiding emotions | -3 | 4 |
| can be trusted/cannot be trusted | -4 | -1 |
| always right/makes mistakes | 2 | 1 |
| adapts to needs/rigid in approach | -4 | -1 |
| Problem solves/worries or avoids | -2 | 1 |

The above raw scores indicate that there are many behaviours where the identity would like to see improved behaviour over the long term when acting as me as a professional. The constructs where the most room for improved behaviour are: to be more accepting, struggle to keep boundaries, be more willing to learn, be more creative, and lead to hiding emotions. Lead to hiding emotions, accepts, is willing to learn and struggles to maintain boundaries are core to the identity under investigation. The high-level emotional significance of struggles to maintain boundaries means that the hypothetical identity will likely be aware of the influence that this construct has over the identity. Receptivity toward behaviour change for this, and the remaining core constructs (which have moderate emotional significance) will depend on the degree to which the identity in questions feels that there is sure understanding of them.

There is only one entity at issue regarding contra-identification; a professional I don't admire. Comparison of the raw scores of me as a professional to a professional I don't admire ought to turn up behaviours that the identity of investigation wishes to shun in the workplace (Table 5.4).

For a professional I don't admire, all the constructs are rated negatively. However, not all of them are rated more negatively than me as a professional. Those that are include closed to learning, always right, problem solves. It is recommended that where counselling focuses on this contra-identification pattern, questions be posed that surround the 2 core constructs at issue: worries or avoids, and, is closed to learning. It may also be

Table 5.4 Raw scores: contra-identification

| Construct | Me as a Professional | Professional I Don't Admire |
|---|---|---|
| accepts/judges | -4 | -2 |
| strong boundaries/struggles boundaries | -4 | -4 |
| shares knowledge/doesn't share | -4 | -1 |
| willing to learn/closed to learning | -2 | -4 |
| well informed/ poorly informed | -2 | -2 |
| creative/tried and tested | -3 | -2 |
| challenges/never challenges | -2 | -1 |
| instructs/reflection | -4 | -3 |
| processing emotions/hiding emotions | -3 | -3 |
| can be trusted/cannot be trusted | -4 | -2 |
| always right/makes mistakes | 2 | -4 |
| adapts to needs/rigid in approach | 4 | -2 |
| Problem solves/worries or avoids | -2 | -2 |

worth focusing questions on the conflicted constructs makes mistakes/ always right and adapts to my needs/is quite rigid in approach.

## Empathetic Identifications

*Empathetic Identification: minimum value = 0.00, maximum value = 1.00. Whereas idealistic identifications represent long-term aspirations; empathetic identifications are of the here and now. Change in empathetic identifications across context and mood states reflects potential for change in behaviour.*

Current empathetic identifications based on 'me as a professional' are: a professional I don't admire (0.92), key adult female (0.69)

Current empathetic identifications based on 'me outside of work' are: key adult female (0.92),

Past empathetic identifications based on 'me as a trainee' are: a professional I don't admire (1.00), key adult female (0.77)

In the above, we see changes in empathetic identification over time. That is, the identity in current times feels slightly less like a professional I don't admire and key female figure than was the case in the past. Outside work we see a dramatic shift in that a professional I don't admire is not an entity of empathetic identification. Further, we see that outside work is where behaviours are seen to most emulate the admired key adult female. It is to be noted that a professional I don't admire is an entity of contraidentification. The findings for empathetic identification support the argument for counselling around this contra-identification pattern.

## Conflicted Identification

*Conflicted identification: minimum value = 0.00, maximum value = 1.00*
*Conflicted identification in ISA references the combination of contra- and empathetic identification with significant others; being 'as' another while at the same time wishing to disassociate from those characteristics that are seen to be held in common.*

Current conflicted identification-conflicts based on 'me as a professional' are: a professional I don't admire (0.96), key adult male(0.73), a person I no longer like (065), a public figure I admire (0.65)

Current conflicted identification based on 'me outside of work' are: none

Past conflicted identification based on 'me as a trainee' are:: a professional I don't admire (1.00), key adult male(0.77), a person I no longer like (0.69), a public figure I admire (0.69)

Table 5.5 indicates that several constructs are involved in the conflicted identification pattern across the entities of conflicted identification. We will focus upon those at issue in particular: strong boundaries/struggles with boundaries, willing to learn/closed to learning, well informed/poorly informed, can be trusted/cannot be trusted. It is the case that all 4 of these constructs are core to the identity in question and that the construct, willing to learn/closed to learning was at issue in the contra identification pattern with a professional I don't admire. Focus counselling on these constructs in order to help the hypothetical identity overcome the conflicted identifications. Focus in particular on willing to learn/closed to learning.

## EVALUATION OF AND EGO INVOLVEMENT WITH OTHERS

*Evaluation minimum value = -1.00 maximum value = +1.00*
*Ego involvement minimum value = 0.00 maximum value = 5.00*
*Evaluation of others refers to a summation of the positive and negative scores associated with each entity. Entities as a result can have a positive or negative value for this parameter.*
*Ego involvement refers to the overall responsiveness to an entity in terms of the extensiveness in quantity (number of characteristics possessed) and strength (where the rating of each characteristic lies along the zero-centre scale) of the attributes they are rated as possessing.*

## ENTITIES OF PRIMARY INVESTIGATIVE INTEREST

A professional I don't admire (evaluation of -0.78) (ego involvement: 3.40)
Key adult female (evaluation of 0.95) (ego involvement: 5.00)
A public figure I admire (evaluation of -0.82) (ego: 4.36)
A person I no longer like (evaluation of -0.51) (ego: 4.57)

This identity exhibits moderate evaluation of all entities of investigative interest other than key adult female (high evaluation). Similarly, there is moderate ego involvement with all the entities of investigative interest other than key adult female with whom ego involvement is maximal. This

**Table 5.5** Raw scores: conflicted identification

| Construct | Me as a Professional | A Professional I Don't Admire | A Person I no Longer Like | A Public figure I Admire |
|---|---|---|---|---|
| accepts/judges | -4 | -2 | -3 | -4 |
| strong boundaries/struggles boundaries | -4 | -4 | -4 | -4 |
| shares knowledge/doesn't share | -4 | -1 | -3 | 1 |
| willing to learn/closed to learning | -2 | -4 | -4 | -4 |
| well informed/ poorly informed | -2 | -2 | -4 | -4 |
| creative/tried and tested | -3 | -2 | 2 | -4 |
| challenges/never challenges | -2 | -1 | -4 | 3 |
| instructs/reflection | -4 | -3 | 1 | 1 |
| processing emotions/hiding emotions | -3 | -3 | 4 | -4 |
| can be trusted/cannot be trusted | -4 | -2 | -2 | -4 |
| always right/makes mistakes | 2 | -4 | -4 | -4 |
| adapts to needs/rigid in approach | -4 | -2 | 4 | 0 |
| Problem solves/worries or avoids | -2 | -2 | -4 | -4 |

identity is motivated to behave as per the perceived behaviours of key adult female.

## EVALUATION OF SELF, EXTENT OF IDENTITY DIFFUSION, AND IDENTITY VARIANT

*Self-evaluation: minimum value = -1.00, maximum value = 1.00*
*Identity Diffusion: minimum value = 0.00, maximum value = 1.00*
*Self-evaluation refers to measurements wherein characteristics associated with the various entities of self (me as a student teacher, me at work etc.) are compared to characteristics associated with the ideal aspirational self (me as I would like to be).*
*Identity diffusion in ISA is a measure of the extent of a person's conflicts of identification* (Fig. 5.1).

**'Me as I would like to be'**
Self-evaluation: 0.83
Identity diffusion: 0.31
Identity variant: Confident

5 THE CRISIS VARIANT    101

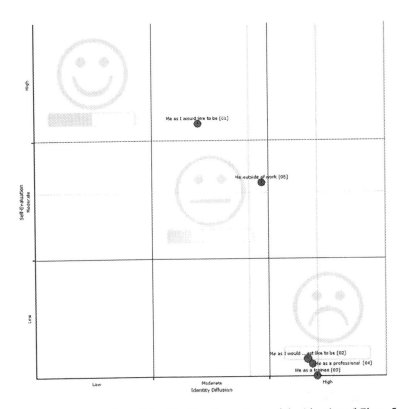

**Fig. 5.1** Representation of the ISA identity variants of the identity of Chap. 5

*'Me as I would least like to be'*
Self-evaluation: −0.83
Identity diffusion: 0.60
Identity Variant: Crisis
*'Me, as trainee'*
Self-evaluation: −1.00
Identity diffusion: 0.65
Identity variant: Crisis
*'Me, as a professional'*
Self–evaluation: 0.88

Identity Diffusion: 0.63
Identity Variant: Crisis
***Me, outside of work***
Self-evaluation: 0.99
Identity Diffusion: 0.40
Identity Variant: Indeterminate

Me as I would like to be is rated high (confident). This might be seen as a hopeful finding as it suggests that despite the current crisis, the identity sees room for improvement. However, a counsellor would be wise to avoid trying to mentor self toward more realistic expectations for future behaviours until the crisis is resolved. There are fully three entities of self that are rated in crisis. That is, in these arenas, the identity recognises a high level of conflicted identifications and has a tendency for low self-evaluation. Counselling to improve the self-evaluation of the three entities of self in crisis is recommended (see the earlier suggestions for tackling the conflicted and contra-identification patterns). Me outside work is rated indeterminate, suggesting that this hypothetical identity feels better about self when outside work.

## Summary of ISA Report

The core constructs of this identity are: struggles to keep boundaries, is willing to learn, worries or avoids, can be trusted, is well informed, accepts, leads to hiding emotions. Is willing to learn, and is well informed are formative constructs, struggles to keep boundaries and can be trusted are normative and accepts, leads to processing emotions and problem solves are restorative. Interestingly, unlike the identities in Chaps. 2 and 3, this identity has a mix of core constructs across the three themes. Struggles to maintain boundaries is associated with maximal emotional significance. The emotional significance of the remaining core constructs is moderate. There is good potential that the identity is aware that struggles to maintain boundaries influences behaviour. As highlighted through the discussion of the other identities of this text, maintaining boundaries is an essential skill of a counsellor. By highlighting this as a potential concern, the ISA analysis can allow for this to be discussed and addressed within supervision with the support of an experienced counsellor. It may or may not be the case that the identity is aware of the constructs that are associated with moderate emotional significance. Addressing the other core constructs within supervision may also support the supervisee to consider the skills they have that are required in the counselling profession to uncover any concerns they may have.

The conflicted constructs are: makes mistakes, shares knowledge, adapts to my needs, and challenges. Shares knowledge is formative, challenges and makes mistakes are normative, and, adapts to my needs is restorative. All of the conflicted constructs are associated with moderate emotional significance and as such the identity may not be aware that they represent issues. We recommend that counselling supervision begins with questioning around the most stressed construct. A suitable opening question might be 'can you speak of situations where you have struggled over whether to mount a challenge or not?' Thereafter, draw up plans to help the hypothetical identity manage behaviours around this construct and monitor those behaviours. The same approach to questioning could be applied to remaining conflicted constructs. The supervisor could also highlight the attributes of a counsellor that sharing knowledge is ok and discuss the benefits of appropriate self-disclosure within a counselling setting. Support and guidance within the supervision session around self-disclosure may help resolve the conflict with this particular construct. Likewise, discussion around the other constructs may help the supervisee understand and manage issues they have with these constructs and open up in order to resolve their concerns. To associate a conflicted construct with a core or pressured construct, consider the construct challenges/never challenges and the construct has strong boundaries/struggles to keep boundaries. A suitable question might be 'is it the case that never challenging a situation or situations can interfere with your ability to maintain boundaries'. After posing the question, conduct discussion around it.

There is strong positive identification with the key adult female and a good friend. Raw scores of me as a professional and a professional I admire indicate behaviours the identity would like to improve, like behaviour over the long term whilst in the workplace. This comparison turned up to be more accepting, struggle to keep boundaries, be more willing to learn, be more creative, and lead to hiding emotions. Other than being more creative, these constructs are core. Receptivity to counselling supervision toward core constructs will depend upon the degree to which the identity is sure of the stance toward them.

There is only one entity at issue regarding contra-identification, a professional I don't admire. For this entity, the constructs at issue are: closed to learning, always right, problem solves. Pose questions around these constructs during counselling supervision to uncover the source of associated issues. These are interesting to explore through supervision, but it is also interesting that these attributes are not necessarily valued within the counselling profession, so this could be the reason they do not admire this professional. Linking to theory, this could represent an identity deficit, with the individual struggling with their personal goals and values (Baumeister et al., 1985).

Regarding empathetic identification, the hypothetical identity in current times feels slightly less like a professional I don't admire and key adult female than was the case in the past. Outside work, a professional I don't admire is not an entity of empathetic identification and there is greater emulation of the behaviours of key adult female. Note that a professional I don't admire is the object of contra-identification. The findings for empathetic identification support counselling supervision, around contra-identification with a professional I don't admire.

The entities of conflicted identification at work in past and current times are: a professional I don't admire, key adult male, a person I no longer like and a public figure I admire. There are no conflicted identifications outside work. Several constructs are involved in the conflicted identifications of the work domain: strong boundaries/struggles with boundaries, willing to learn/closed to learning, well informed/poorly informed, can be trusted/cannot be trusted. All 4 of these constructs are core to the identity in question and the construct, willing to learn/closed to learning is at issue in the contra-identification pattern. Focus on these constructs within supervision and focus in particular on willing to learn/closed to learning.

The entities of investigative interest are: a professional I don't admire. Key adult female, a public figure I admire, a person I no longer like. There is moderate evaluation of all these entities other than key adult female (high evaluation). Similarly, there is moderate ego involvement with all the entities of investigative interest other than key adult female (maximal ego involvement). This is an identity motivated to behave as per the perceived behaviours of key adult female.

Regarding identity variants, me as I would like to be is rated too high (confident). This can be seen as a hopeful finding as it suggests that despite the current crisis, the identity sees room for improvement. This is an important insight for the supervision process and suggests the identity can benefit a lot from understanding more about themselves through the guidance of a more experienced counselling professional. Supervision will hopefully help with the over-confidence, which is perhaps a defence mechanism, and uncover why they have this over-confidence. This identity needs supervision guidance to maintain them in the profession and provide them with a more productive identification as a counselling professional. Indeed, identity development theorists view identity crisis resolution as an important function, allowing for a more superior identity once a resolution has occurred (Baumeister et al., 1985). Three entities of self that are rated in crisis. Counselling supervision to improve self-evaluation of these entities of self (see the earlier suggestions for tackling the conflicted and contra-identification patterns). Me outside work is rated indeterminate, suggesting this person feels better about self when outside work. This is yet another important insight from the ISA process to support and address within the supervision process in order to develop the counselling skills of the identity to move them into a more secure and positive identification within the profession.

## References

Baumeister, R. F., Shapiro, J. P., & Tice, D. M. (1985). Two kinds of identity crisis. *Journal of Personality, 53*, 407–424.

Erikson, E. (1956). The problem of ego identity. *Journal of the American Psychoanalytic Association.* https://doi.org/10.1177/000306515600400104

Erikson, E. (1968). *Identity, youth and crisis.* Norton.

Kernberg, O. (1978). The diagnosis of borderline conditions in adolescence. *Adolescent Psychiatry, 6*, 298–319. Edited by: Feinstein, S., Giovacchini, P. 1978, Chicago: University of Chicago Press.

Schwartz, S. J. (2001). The evolution of Eriksonian and, neo-Eriksonian identity theory and research: A review and integration. *Identity: An International Journal of theory and Research, 1*(1), 7–58. https://doi.org/10.1207/S1532706XSCHWARTZ

# CHAPTER 6

# The Defensive Negative Variant

**Abstract** Here we present a final illustrative ISA analysis. This time for the defensive negative identity variant. The approach to presenting the analysis is the same as prior chapters.

**Keywords** Defensive negative identity variant • Identity content valence theory • Negative identity • Positive identity • PDP • mHealth • Supervision • Mentoring

## Introduction

This last chapter will present another dimension on the ISA grid: the defensive negative variant. Erikson (1968) posited that identities consist of both positive and negative sides and that negative identities are not identities lacking positive attributes. Rather, a negative identity develops through the individual identifying with roles opposing expectations from society and consists of negative aspects of the self. According to identity content valence theory, a negative identity chooses negative roles and renounces positive ones (Kroger & Marcia, 2011). Identity research tends to focus on more positive identities rather than negative identities or identities in crisis. This chapter will consider a negative identity in terms of a defensive negative variant.

© The Author(s), under exclusive license to Springer Nature Switzerland AG 2022
G. Passmore, J. Prescott, *Using an ISA Mobile App for Professional Development*, https://doi.org/10.1007/978-3-030-99071-8_6

Throughout this publication, we have provided the reader with an understanding of what ISA is, how to use the app and examples of four contrasting identity variants the ISA method can expose for support. One of the premises of the book is to build on our previous work (Passmore et al., 2019) that proposed combining ISA with a mentoring approach to support trainee teachers by suggesting ISA can support trainee and qualified counsellors through supervision. The aim is to take a look at how ISA can help guide a counselling supervisor to support a supervisee and highlight areas of support the supervisee may not be aware of or want to acknowledge. Although this book has focused on counselling supervision, the process can be applied to other professionals where supervision is required (e.g. social work). We also posit that the process is good for general PDP since the aim of ISA is to help an individual gain insight they may or may not be fully aware of and can develop from knowing. As highlighted in Chap. 1, an ISA instrument can be developed by researchers and professionals in any given area, as long as the instrument designer has insight into the requisite professional needs in order to support supervision or a PDP process.

## STRUCTURAL PRESSURE AND EMOTIONAL SIGNIFICANCE

*Emotional Significance: Minimum value = 0.00, maximum value = 100.00*
The emotional significance of a construct used in the appraisal of the counsellor's social world is defined as the strength of affect associated with the expression of the construct. The index of standardised emotional significance can range from 0.00 (no significance) to 10.00 (maximal significance).

*Structural Pressure: Minimum value = -100, maximum value = +100*
Structural Pressure reflects the consistency with which a construct is used to evaluate entities. High Structural Pressure constructs are used in a consistent manner to evaluate others. They represent the core, stable evaluative dimensions of the identity under consideration. Low Structural Pressure constructs are used to evaluate others in different ways depending on circumstance and context. Low Structural Pressure suggests an area of stress and indecision; a conflicted dimension liable to poor decision making (Table 6.1).

Core constructs concern: struggles to keep boundaries, leads to hiding emotions, instructs, accepts. These constructs are distributed across 2 of

**Table 6.1** Core and conflicted values and beliefs

| Pole 1 | Pole 2 | SP | ES |
|---|---|---|---|
| Core constructs | | | |
| has strong boundaries | *struggles to keep boundaries* | 100.00 | 10.00 |
| facilitates processing emotions | *leads to hiding* | 86.59 | 8.66 |
| Instructs | encourages reflection | 75.96 | 7.60 |
| Accepts | Judges | 70.79 | 7.08 |
| Conflicted constructs | | | |
| *is willing to learn* | closed to learning | -4.19 | 7.57 |
| *problem solves* | worries or avoids | -16.78 | 8.13 |

the themes of the instrument. Struggles to keep boundaries and instructs are normative, and, hiding emotions and accepts are restorative.

Struggles to keep boundaries is pressured and the remaining constructs are core. Struggles to keep boundaries is associated with maximal emotional significance; leads to hiding emotions is a construct of high emotional significance. The emotional significance of the remaining core constructs is moderate. The pressured construct, struggles to maintain boundaries, is a pivotal black and white issue for this identity. That the associated emotional significance is maximal, indicates there may be an acute awareness of the influence it holds over behaviour. It is likely that there will be an awareness of the influence of leads to hiding emotions. There may or may not be an awareness of instructs and accepts.

The conflicted constructs are: is willing to learn and problem solves. Is willing to learn is formative, and problem solves is restorative. No one theme dominates the conflicted constructs and can thus be considered a prime target for counselling. None of the conflicted constructs are sufficiently stressed as to merit a contradictory ISA rating. All of the conflicted constructs are associated with moderate emotional significance and as such the identity may or may not be aware that they represent issues. The tack we recommend for counselling then is to begin with questions around the most stressed construct. A suitable opening question might be 'do you find yourself worrying about certain problems or setting about solving them?' With the question answered, draw up plans to improve behaviour around the construct and monitor subsequent behaviour. Apply the same approach to questioning and planning to the remaining conflicted constructs.

To associate a conflicted construct with a core or pressured construct, consider the construct problem solves/worries or avoids and the construct has strong boundaries/struggles to keep boundaries. A suitable question might be 'does your stance toward solving problems or worrying about them impact with your ability to maintain boundaries'. After posing the question, begin a discussion around it so that plans for improved behaviours can be developed.

## IDEALISTIC AND CONTRA-IDENTIFICATIONS

*Idealistic Identification: minimum value = 0.00, maximum value = 1.00*
*Contra-Identification: minimum value = 0.00, maximum value = 1.00*
*Idealistic identifications (II) point to a person's role models. They indicate the characteristics a person will seek to emulate over the long term.*
*Contra-identifications (CI) indicate negative role models. Those who possess characteristics from which a person wishes to dissociate* (Table 6.2).

The hypothetical identity of this chapter exhibits strong positive identification with a person I no longer like and a good friend. Looking at raw scores, differences in the behaviours seen in 'me as a professional' and 'a professional I admire' is unlikely to reveal long-term aspirant behaviours as the latter entity is an entity of contra-identification. We turn then to a comparison of me as a professional to a good friend (Table 6.3).

The above raw scores indicate that there are many behaviours where the identity would like to see improved behaviour over the long term when acting as me as a professional. The constructs where the most room for improved behaviour are seen are: to more often struggle to keep boundaries, to instruct more, can be trusted, and to solve problems more often. Struggling to keep boundaries and instructs are core to the identity

**Table 6.2** Idealistic and contra-identifications

| Entity | II | CI |
| --- | --- | --- |
| A person I no longer like | 1.00 | |
| A good friend | 0.92 | |
| Professional I admire | | 0.23 |
| Public figure I admire | | 0.23 |
| Public figure I don't admire | | 0.23 |
| Key adult male | | 0.23 |

**Table 6.3** Raw scores: idealistic identification

| Construct | Me as a Professional | A Good Friend |
|---|---|---|
| accepts/judges | -1 | 1 |
| strong boundaries/struggles boundaries | -3 | 4 |
| shares knowledge/doesn't share | -3 | -2 |
| willing to learn/closed to learning | 4 | 2 |
| well informed/ poorly informed | -2 | 1 |
| creative/tried and tested | -2 | 2 |
| challenges/never challenges | -3 | 1 |
| instructs/reflection | -4 | 3 |
| processing emotions/hiding emotions | -2 | 4 |
| can be trusted/cannot be trusted | -4 | 1 |
| always right/makes mistakes | 0 | 2 |
| adapts to needs/rigid in approach | 2 | 4 |
| Problem solves/worries or avoids | -1 | 4 |

in question. The issue of problem solving or worrying or avoiding is the most conflicted of the constructs. The high-level emotional significance of struggles to maintain boundaries means and the pressured status suggest that attempts to mentor toward improved behaviours regarding this core construct will be rebuffed. Receptivity toward behaviour change regarding instructs/reflects will depend on whether there is awareness of the construct given its moderate emotional significance. An approach to counselling to increase the frequency of problem solving has been considered in the conflicted constructs section of this analysis.

There are multiple entities of contra-identification. Comparison of raw scores across these entities may turn up behaviours that the identity under investigation wishes to shun in the workplace.

In the case of me as a professional, all the constructs except 'willing to learn and adapts to needs' have a negative raw score. The prevalence of such negative ratings for an entity of self, points to a problem for this identity. One construct (relative to me as a professional) is more negative for all of the entities of contra-identification in Table 6.4, problem solves/worries or avoids. Recall that this construct is the most conflicted construct for this hypothetical identity. It is recommended that counselling for contra-identification focuses on the issue of increasing behaviours that promote problem solving (a long-term aspirant behaviour).

**Table 6.4** Raw scores: contra-identification

| Construct | Me as Professional | Professional Admire | Public Admire | Public Don't Admire | Key Adult Male |
|---|---|---|---|---|---|
| accepts/judges | -1 | 1 | 1 | 4 | 3 |
| strong boundaries/struggles boundaries | -3 | 1 | 1 | 4 | 4 |
| shares knowledge/doesn't share | -3 | -1 | 3 | -1 | 2 |
| willing to learn/closed to learning | 4 | 0 | 2 | 2 | -4 |
| well informed/ poorly informed | -2 | 0 | 1 | 2 | 1 |
| creative/tried and tested | -2 | 3 | 2 | -4 | 3 |
| challenges/never challenges | -3 | 3 | -4 | 2 | -4 |
| instructs/reflection | -4 | 0 | 1 | 0 | 3 |
| processing emotions/hiding emotions | -2 | 4 | 3 | 4 | 1 |
| can be trusted/cannot be trusted | -4 | -1 | 0 | 4 | 1 |
| always right/makes mistakes | 0 | 1 | 3 | 4 | 1 |
| adapts to needs/rigid in approach | 2 | 0 | -1 | 4 | 2 |
| Problem solves/worries or avoids | -1 | -2 | -2 | -4 | -3 |

## EMPATHETIC IDENTIFICATIONS

*Empathetic Identification: minimum value = 0.00, maximum value = 1.00*
*Whereas idealistic identifications represent long-term aspirations, empathetic identifications are of the here and now. Change in empathetic identifications across context and mood states reflects the potential for change in behaviour.*

Current empathetic identifications based on 'me as a professional' are: none
Current empathetic identifications based on 'me outside of work' are: none
Past empathetic identifications based on 'me as a trainee' are: none

It is the case that there are no significant empathetic identifications for this identity. However, there is moderate empathetic identification for a public figure I don't admire in the case of me as a professional. Also present at a moderate level (but to a lesser degree) for me as a professional is empathetic identification with a public figure I admire, a public figure I don't admire, key adult male and a good friend. Recall that a good friend is the subject of idealistic identification and the public figures (that are and aren't admired) and key adult male are the subject of contra-identification. Similar moderate empathetic identification was present for the same entities in the past and outside work but for a public figure I don't admire, this pattern it was less prevalent.

The lack of high-level empathetic identification suggests that for the most part there is little potential to change behaviour over time and across the domains of the instrument. There is, though, a tendency to feel more like a public figure I don't admire in the workplace in present times. However, given the moderate nature of the latter empathetic identification, the extent to which the identity under investigation feels he or she changes behaviour as per this entity of contra-identification is likely limited.

## Conflicted Identification

*Conflicted identification: minimum value = 0.00, maximum value = 1.00*
*Conflicted identification in ISA references the combination of contra- and empathetic identification with significant others; being 'as' another while at the same time wishing to disassociate from those characteristics that are seen to be held in common.*
Current conflicted identification conflicts based on 'me as a professional' are: a public figure I don't admire (0.31)
Current conflicted identification based on 'me outside of work' are: none
Past conflicted identification based on 'me as a trainee' are: none

Outside work and in work in the past there are no entities of conflicted identification. In present times a public figure I don't admire has become an entity of potentially troublesome identification. Table 6.5 reveals something of the nature of this conflicted identification.

Several constructs are involved in the conflicted identification pattern of Table 6.5. Share knowledge/doesn't share knowledge, creative/tried and tested, problem solves/worries or avoids. Not one of these constructs is core to the identity in question but solves problems/worries or avoids it is the most conflicted of the constructs, and it is implicated in the idealistic and contra-identification patterns. The latter statement reinforces the need to counsel toward improved behaviour regarding the construct, problem solving.

**Table 6.5** Raw scores: conflicted identification

| Construct | Me as a Professional | A Public Figure I Don't Admire |
|---|---|---|
| accepts/judges | -1 | 4 |
| strong boundaries/struggles boundaries | -3 | 4 |
| shares knowledge/doesn't share | -3 | -1 |
| willing to learn/closed to learning | 4 | 2 |
| well informed/ poorly informed | -2 | 2 |
| creative/tried and tested | -2 | -4 |
| challenges/never challenges | -3 | 2 |
| instructs/reflection | -4 | 0 |
| processing emotions/hiding emotions | -2 | 4 |
| can be trusted/cannot be trusted | -4 | 4 |
| always right/makes mistakes | 0 | 4 |
| adapts to needs/rigid in approach | 2 | 4 |
| Problem solves/worries or avoids | -1 | -4 |

## Evaluation of and Ego Involvement with Others

*Evaluation minimum value = -1.00 maximum value = +1.00*
*Ego involvement minimum value = 0.00 maximum value = 5.00*
*Evaluation of others refers to a summation of the positive and negative scores associated with each entity. Entities as a result can have a positive or negative value for this parameter.*
*Ego involvement refers to the overall responsiveness to an entity in terms of the extensiveness in quantity (number of characteristics possessed) and strength (where the rating of each characteristic lies along the zero-centre scale) of the attributes they are rated as possessing.*

## Entities of Primary Investigative Interest

A person I no longer like (evaluation of 0.92) (ego: 4.02)
A good friend (evaluation of 0.75) (ego: 3.78)
A professional I admire (evaluation of 0.36) (ego: 2.07)

A public figure I admire (evaluation of 0.30) (ego: 2.93)
A public figure I don't admire (evaluation of 0.63) (ego: 4.76)
Key adult male (evaluation of 0.28) (ego involvement: 3.90)

This identity exhibits moderate evaluation for all entities of investigative interest. There is moderate ego involvement with all the entities of investigative interest other than a public figure I don't admire. Across the entities of investigative interest, this identity is motivated, to the greatest degree, to behave as per a public figure I don't admire.

## Evaluation of Self, Extent of Identity Diffusion, and Identity Variant

*Self-evaluation: minimum value = -1.00, maximum value = 1.00*
*Identity Diffusion: minimum value = 0.00, maximum value = 1.00*
*Self-evaluation refers to measurements wherein characteristics associated with the various entities of self (me as a student teacher, me at work etc.) are compared to characteristics associated with the ideal aspirational self (me as I would like to be).*
*Identity diffusion in ISA is a measure of the extent of a person's conflicts of identification.*

**'Me as I would like to be'**
Self-evaluation:   1.00
Identity diffusion:        0.29
Identity variant: Confident

**'Me as I would least like to be'**
Self-evaluation:   -0.81
Identity diffusion:        0.17
Identity Variant: Defensive Negative

**'Me, as trainee'**
Self-evaluation: -0.53
Identity diffusion: 0.17
Identity variant: Defensive Negative

**'Me, as a professional'**
Self-evaluation: -0.57
Identity Diffusion: 0.22
Identity Variant: Defensive Negative

**'Me, outside of work**
Self-evaluation: −0.69
Identity Diffusion: 0.19
Identity Variant: Defensive Negative

It is the case that 4 of the 5 entities of self are rated defensive negative. Me as I would like to be is rated too high (confident), which suggests that despite the current low self-evaluation of remaining entities of self, there is hope for future improvement in behaviour. In addition to low self-evaluation, the defensive negative variants fail to fully recognise conflicted identifications, hence the bottom left location of most of the entities in Fig. 6.1. Counselling to improve the self-evaluation of the defensive

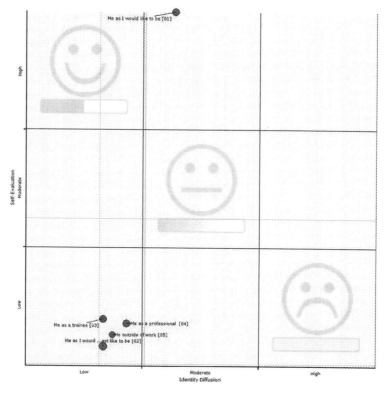

**Fig. 6.1** Representation of the ISA identity variants of the identity of Chap. 6

negative entities of self is recommended. Also recommended is counselling to increase capacity to recognise and deal with conflicted identifications. Suggestions for tackling the conflicted and contra-identification patterns are available in earlier sections of this analysis.

## Summary of ISA Report

The core constructs of this identity concern: struggles to keep boundaries, leads to hiding emotions, instructs, accepts. These constructs are distributed across 2 of the themes of the instrument. Struggles to keep boundaries and instructs are constructs in the normative function, and, hiding emotions and accepts are restorative functions. Struggles to keep boundaries is pressured and the remaining constructs are core. Struggles to keep boundaries is associated with maximal emotional significance. Leads to hiding emotions is a construct of high emotional significance. The emotional significance of the remaining core constructs is moderate. The pressured construct, struggles to maintain boundaries is a pivotal black and white issue for this identity. That the associated emotional significance is maximal indicates there may be acute awareness of the influence it holds over behaviour. It is likely that there will be awareness of the influence of leads to hiding emotions. There may or may not be awareness of instructs and accepts. These are important insights to address within supervision for promoting the ability to keep boundaries, being accepting and non-instructive are important skills for a counsellor to develop. Note please that this person may not be suitable for a career in counselling if they cannot work on these core constructs of their identity. They are constructs that conflict with the identity of a counselling professional. Within supervision is the ideal safe environment for the discussions of these PDP issues to be considered.

The conflicted constructs are: is willing to learn and problem solves. Is willing to learn is formative and problem solves is restorative. No one theme dominates the conflicted constructs and no conflicted construct is sufficiently stressed as to merit a contradictory ISA rating. All of the conflicted constructs are associated with moderate emotional significance and as such the identity may or may not be aware that they represent issues. We recommend questioning the most stressed construct. A suitable opening question might be 'do you find yourself worrying about certain problems or setting about solving them?' With the question answered, draw up plans to improve behaviour around the construct and monitor subsequent behaviour. Apply the same approach to questioning and planning for the remaining conflicted constructs.

To associate a conflicted construct with a core or pressured construct, consider the construct problem solves/worries or avoids and the construct has strong boundaries/struggles to keep boundaries. A suitable question might be 'does your stance toward solving problems or worrying about them impact with your ability to maintain boundaries'. After posing the question, begin discussion around it so that plans for improved behaviours, and how can the supervision process can support this, can be developed.

There is strong positive identification with a person I no longer like and a good friend. Raw scores comparing me as a professional and 'a professional I admire' are unlikely to reveal long-term aspirant behaviours as the latter entity is an entity of contra-identification. We turn then to a comparison of me as a professional and a good friend. Here raw scores indicate that there are many behaviours where the identity would like to see improved behaviour over the long term when acting as me as a professional. The constructs where the most room for improved behaviour are seen are: to more often struggle to keep boundaries, to instruct more, to be more trusted, and to solve problems more often. Struggling to keep boundaries and instructs are core to the identity in question. Mentoring toward core constructs is often rejected as an understanding of them is considered to be significant by the client. Receptivity toward behaviour change regarding instructs/reflects will depend on whether there is awareness of the construct, given its moderate emotional significance. A counselling supervision approach to increase the frequency of problem solving has been considered earlier in this analysis.

Concerning contra-identification, me as a professional, exhibits negative raw scores across most all constructs of the instrument, which in and of itself points to a problem for this identity. One construct stands out as more negative for the entities of contra-identification; problem solves/worries or avoids. This is also the most conflicted construct and it is recommended that counselling focus on increasing behaviours that promote successful problem solving (a long-term aspirant behaviour).

No significant empathetic identifications were found for this identity. There is moderate empathetic identification for a public figure I don't admire in the case of me as a professional. Also present is moderate (but to a lesser degree) empathetic identification for me as a professional with: a public figure I admire, a public figure I don't admire, key adult male and a good friend. Recall that a good friend is the subject of idealistic identification and the public figures (that are and aren't admired) and key adult male are the subject of contra-identification. Similar moderate empathetic identification was present for the same entities in the past and outside work but for a public figure I don't admire, this pattern was less prevalent. For the most part, there is little potential to change behaviour over time and across the domains of the instrument. There is a tendency to feel more like a public figure I don't admire in the workplace in present times. However, given the moderate nature of the latter empathetic identification, the extent to which the identity under investigation feels he or she behaves as per this entity of contra-identification is likely limited.

Outside work and in work in the past, there are no entities of conflicted identification. In present times, a public figure I don't admire is an entity of potential troublesome identification. Several constructs are involved in this conflicted identification pattern: share knowledge/doesn't share knowledge, creative/tried and tested, challenges/never challenges, problem solves/worries or avoids. These constructs are not core to the identity in question, but solves problems/worries or avoids is the most conflicted construct. The latter construct is also implicated in the idealistic and contra-identification patterns of this identity. The latter statement reinforces the need to counsel toward improved behaviour regarding problem solving.

The entities of investigative interest are: a person I no longer like, a good friend, a professional I admire, a public figure I admire, a public figure I don't admire, and, key adult male. This hypothetical identity exhibits moderate evaluation of all entities of investigative interest. There is moderate ego involvement with all the entities of investigative interest other than a public figure I don't admire. Across the entities of investigative interest, this identity is motivated, to the greatest degree, to behave as per a public figure I don't admire.

Four of the 5 entities of self are rated defensive negative. Me as I would like to be is rated confident, which suggests that there is hope for future improvement in behaviour. In addition to low self-evaluation, the defensive negative variants fail to fully recognise conflicted identifications. Supervision to improve the self-evaluation of these defensive negative entities of self is recommended. Also recommended is supervision to increase capacity to recognise and deal with conflicted identifications. Suggestions for tackling the conflicted and contra-identification patterns are available in earlier sections of this analysis.

## Concluding Comments and Thoughts

To conclude this publication, we thought we would return to technology since one of the aims of this publication is to showcase the use of a newly developed ISA smartphone application. These concluding comments will discuss how technology can support supervision. We will also discuss the use of ISA and the ISA app for supervision and professional development support across a range of disciplines.

## Technology Support

There is an increasing abundance of smartphone applications being used in all aspects of our lives. In particular, recent years have witnessed a strong move in the implementation of mHealth smartphone applications, and this includes the use of smartphone applications to support those working in health care professions. For instance, mHealth resources have been utilised to support the nursing role and improve knowledge bases (Ronquillo et al., 2019; Ferguson et al., 2019; Chang et al., 2021), improve the maternity services offered by midwives (White et al., 2019; Arnaert et al., 2020) and undertake tasks carried out by general practitioners (Wattanapisit et al., 2020). Aside from patient care improvements, smartphone applications have also been highlighted as a potential use in the reduction of stress (Hwang & Jo, 2019) and burnout (Heeter et al., 2017; Wood et al., 2017) of clinical staff. Although these apps were not directly related to clinical supervision, it is evident that through a reduction of stress and burnout, the apps support clinical professionals in their careers and this information is useful from a PDP and supervision perspective.

## ISA for Professional Development Across Disciplines

Supervision can play an important role in reducing stress, and burnout (Love et al., 2017; Johnson et al., 2020), as well as retaining a health workforce, through increasing the well-being of staff (Oates, 2018). Clinical supervision has been defined as '*the provision of guidance of clinical practice for qualified health professionals by a more experienced health professional*' (Snowdon et al., 2017, p. 2). This form of supervision may help staff to minimise any lack in their own knowledge and ensure a higher quality of patient care. In terms of the benefits of the ISA in our first publication (Passmore et al., 2019), we highlighted how ISA can be used in conjunction with mentoring to support trainee teachers, to reduce stress, burnout and support retention through a strong identification with the teaching profession. In this publication, we hoped to provide the reader with a thorough understanding of the newly developed and freely accessible mobile app we have developed, as well as how one might read and interpret an ISA report, using the example of counselling supervision. An extended aim of this publication is to show the reader that we believe the ISA approach can support a PDP process in any given career setting. That is, ISA can be used in conjunction with mentoring, as was the case with the trainee teacher example, or, as we have used throughout this publication, as part of the supervision process of a trainee. In fact, ISA and mentoring can be used to provide PDP for qualified counsellors. Further, as noted in the Introduction, we wish to advocate that the ISA and mentoring process can be useful to provide insights within any profession and that it is useful for any clinical and non-clinical supervision process.

## References

Arnaert, A. L., Ponzoni, N., Debe, Z., Meda, M. M., Nana, N. G., & Arnaert, S. (2020). Experiences of midwives and community health workers using mHealth to improve services to pregnant women in rural Burkina Faso, Africa. *Journal of Nursing Education and Practice, 10*(3). https://doi.org/10.5430/jnep.v10n3p57

Chang, O., Patel, V. L., Iyengar, S., & May, W. (2021). Impact of a mobile-based (mHealth) tool to support community health nurses in early identification of depression and suicide risk in Pacific Island countries. *Australasian Psychiatry, 29*(2), 200–203. https://doi.org/10.1177/1039856220956458

Erikson, E. H. (1968). *Identity: Youth and crisis*. Norton.

Ferguson, C., Hickman, L. D., Phillips, J., Newton, P. J., Inglis, S. C., Lam, L., & Bajorek, B. V. (2019). An mHealth intervention to improve nurses' atrial fibrillation and anticoagulation knowledge and practice: The EVICOAG study. *European Journal of Cardiovascular Nursing, 18*(1), 7–15. https://doi.org/10.1177/1474515118793051

Heeter, C., Lehto, R., Allbritton, M., Day, T., & Wiseman, M. (2017). Effects of a technology-assisted meditation program on healthcare providers' interoceptive awareness, compassion fatigue, and burnout. *Journal of Hospice & Palliative Nursing, 19*(4), 314–322. https://doi.org/10.1097/NJH.0000000000000349

Hwang, W. J., & Jo, H. H. (2019). Evaluation of the effectiveness of mobile app-based stress-management program: A randomized controlled trial. *International*

*Journal of Environmental Research and Public Health, 16*(21), 4270. https://doi.org/10.3390/ijerph16214270

Johnson, J., Corker, C., & O'connor, D. B. (2020). Burnout in psychological therapists: A cross-sectional study investigating the role of supervisory relationship quality. *Clinical Psychologist, 24*(3), 223–235. https://doi.org/10.1111/cp.12206

Kroger, J., & Marcia, J. E. (2011). The identity statuses: Origins, meanings, and interpretations. In S. J. Schwartz, K. Luyckx, & V. L. Vignoles (Eds.), *Handbook of identity theory and research* (pp. 31–53). Springer.

Love, B., Sidebotham, M., Fenwick, J., Harvey, S., & Fairbrother, G. (2017). "Unscrambling what's in your head": A mixed method evaluation of clinical supervision for midwives. *Women and Birth, 30*(4), 271–281. https://doi.org/10.1016/j.wombi.2016.11.002

Oates, J. (2018). What keeps nurses happy? Implications for workforce well-being strategies. *Nursing Management, 25*(1). https://doi.org/10.7748/nm.2018.e1643

Passmore, G. J., Turner, A., & Prescott, J. (2019). *Identity structure analysis and teacher mentorship: Across the context of schools and the individual.* Palgrave.

Ronquillo, C., Dahinten, V. S., Bungay, V., & Currie, L. M. (2019). The nurse LEADership for implementing technologies-mobile health model (Nurse LEAD-IT-mHealth). *Nursing Leadership (Toronto, Ont.), 32*(2), 71–84. https://doi.org/10.12927/cjnl.2019.25960

Snowdon, D. A., Leggat, S. G., & Taylor, N. F. (2017). Does clinical supervision of healthcare professionals improve effectiveness of care and patient experience? A systematic review. *BMC Health Services Research, 17*(1), 1–11. https://doi.org/10.1186/s12913-017-2739-5

Wattanapisit, A., Teo, C. H., Wattanapisit, S., Teoh, E., Woo, W. J., & Ng, C. J. (2020). Can mobile health apps replace GPs? A scoping review of comparisons between mobile apps and GP tasks. *BMC Medical Informatics and Decision Making, 20*(1), 1–11. https://doi.org/10.1186/s12911-019-1016-4

White, A. H., Crowther, S. A., & Lee, S. H. (2019). Supporting rural midwifery practice using a mobile health (mHealth) intervention: A qualitative descriptive study. *Rural and Remote Health, 19*(3), 5294–5294. https://doi.org/10.22605/rrh5294

Wood, A. E., Prins, A., Bush, N. E., Hsia, J. F., Bourn, L. E., Earley, M. D., Walser, R., & Ruzek, J. (2017). Reduction of burnout in mental health care providers using the provider resilience mobile application. *Community Mental Health Journal, 53*(4), 452–459. https://doi.org/10.1007/s10597-016-0076-5